50 Ways to a Safer World

Everyday Actions You Can Take to Prevent Violence in Neighborhoods, Schools, and Communities

Preface by Deborah Prothrow-Stith, M.D.

Patricia Occhiuzzo Giggans
Barrie Levy

Seal Press
Seattle

Dedication

From Patti: *For Goldie, my father, who taught me that life is a kind of music, and that music is jazz. For Maria, my mother, who taught me that life isn't fair but we must live to make it so.*

From Barrie: *For Faye and Charlie, Nisa and Johanna, and especially Linda, from whom I have learned that when you care to act, and "I" becomes "we," one's world changes.*

Seal Press
3131 Western Avenue, Suite 410
Seattle, Washington 98121
sealprss@scn.org

Library of Congress Cataloging-in-Publication Data
Giggans, Patricia Occhiuzzo.
50 ways to a safer world : everyday actions you can take to prevent violence in neighborhoods, schools, and communities / Patricia Occhiuzzo Giggans, Barrie Levy.
1. Violence—United States—Prevention. 2. Violent crimes—United States—Prevention. 3. School violence—United States—Prevention. 4. Neighborhood watch programs—United States. I. Levy, Barrie. II. Title.
HN90.V5G54   1997   303.6'0973—dc21   97-11673
ISBN 1-878067-95-8

Printed in the United States of America
First printing, July 1997
10 9 8 7 6 5 4 3 2 1

Distributed to the trade by Publishers Group West
In Canada: Publishers Group West Canada, Toronto
In Europe and the U.K.: Airlift Book Company, London
In Australia: Banyan Tree Book Distributors, Kent Town

Cover design by Kate Thompson
Text design by Margaret Flynn
Text composition by Rebecca Engrav and Laura Gronewold

ACKNOWLEDGMENTS

So many contributions from others have gone into this book. The authors wish to acknowledge the people and organizations who have assisted and inspired our work: Leah Aldridge, Cathy Friedman, Sandra Henriquez, Carlos Morales, Manny Velasquez, Jeep Hauser, Kay Hunter and the other staff at the Los Angeles Commission on Assaults Against Women; Ann Reiss Lane from Women Against Gun Violence; Tony Borbon and Billie Weiss from the Violence Prevention Coalition of Greater Los Angeles; Kathy Jett from the California Department of Health Services Office of Women's Health; Bill Martinez; Andrew McGuire of the Pacific Center for Violence Prevention. Special appreciation goes to the bold work and inspired leadership of the California Wellness Foundation's Violence Prevention Initiative and the sixteen Community Action Projects who are on the front lines of violence prevention, and to the Vision of Hope Project of the Crime and Violence Prevention Center of the California Attorney General's Office. Thanks for encouragement from the Boards of Directors of the Statewide California Coalition for Battered Women (SCCBW) and the California Coalition Against Sexual Assault (CalCASA).

Many thanks to everyone at Seal Press for their partnership as we tackled a new arena. Faith Conlon has been a responsive and resourceful editor, giving us creative and thoughtful feedback throughout a lengthy process. Thanks also to Nancy Brandwein who helped to make a tough subject inviting.

Thanks to Ally Giggans who helped with details and Linda Preuss who saved the day when we lost chapters in cyberspace.

Thanks to Ellen Ledley who believed that not only would this project be completed, but constantly reassured us that we were on the right track or gently veered us in the right direction when we weren't. And thanks to Linda Garnets for omelettes and coffee, computer rescues, patience, support and good ideas. Tremendous gratitude goes to our families who put up with this prolonged and demanding effort.

Thanks to the many others, anonymous and unheralded, who every day all across this country, roll up their sleeves and commit to a positive and healthy activism towards peace and nonviolence.

Contents

PART II: SAFETY TO GO   54

PART III: CONCERNS OF OUR TIMES   75

Alcohol/Drugs   76

Youth Violence   90

No Peace in the World without
Peace in the Nations;
No Peace in the Nations without
Peace in the Town;
No Peace in the Town without
Peace in the Home;
No Peace in the Home without
Peace in the Heart.

— from the Tao Te Ching

PREFACE

As a public health professional, medical doctor, former Commissioner of Health of the Commonwealth of Massachusetts, and activist in the field of adolescent violence, I am constantly aware of the heavy toll violence takes on our nation's spirit, health and economy. Violent injury, disability and death consume enormous health care resources and diminish the quality of life of individuals, families and communities. It's time for all of us to take action to prevent this problem. Patricia Occhiuzzo Giggans and Barrie Levy's *50 Ways to a Safer World: Everyday Actions You Can Take to Prevent Violence in Neighborhoods, Schools, and Communities* is an excellent, user-friendly manual to help each of us make our homes and communities safer places to live.

The United States has a problem with violence that is unlike any other country in the world. Our homicide rate for young men is eight times that of Italy, the developed country with the next highest rate, and 100 times greater than the developed country with the lowest rate. The Federal Bureau of Investigation estimates that 1.8 million people in the United States are victims of violence each year. Partner and child abuse plague many of our homes. Schools, the place where young people spend a significant amount of time, are increasingly unable to provide secure settings where learning can take place. Meanwhile, our media glorify violence. We are tired of reading about it in the newspaper. Too many people have suffered the tragic and senseless loss of a family member or friend to violence.

If violence were inevitable—just a part of the human condition—then one would expect the homicide rate from country to country to be relatively similar. When I learned that our homicide rate was so much higher than that of other countries, I was horrified and daunted. Later, I realized that these statistics also revealed an important truth: Violence is preventable. We do not need to have this problem.

Our public policy teaches us to view violence mainly as a criminal justice issue. People believe that building more prisons, lengthening prison sentences, trying children in adult courts and preventing early parole are solutions. The criminal justice system intervenes only after someone has committed an act of violence. We need solutions that prevent violence from happening in the first place as well.

50 Ways to a Safer World is an important and clear guide for actions you can take to prevent violence. Each and every one of us has the power to contribute to making our communities safe. I have had the opportunity to meet thousands of people across the country who are already engaging in violence prevention activities and programs. The magnitude and characteristics of violence-related problems cry out for new and creative approaches. Use some of the fifty ways to change you, your family, community and country. We cannot leave it to others to solve the problem of violence.

Deborah Prothrow-Stith, M.D.
Associate Dean, Harvard School of Public Health
May 1997

INTRODUCTION

This book is our response to fear, helplessness and the sense of powerlessness caused by the pervasive violence that surrounds us all. All over our country, people are worried about violence. Even when violence does not take place in our personal lives, television brings into our living rooms tragedies and crimes as they happen. Easy access to weapons makes violence more lethal and reckless. More young people commit and are victimized by crimes of violence than ever before. Gangs today have proliferated and their members are younger. Parents are worried about the impact of drugs and violence on their children. The prevalence of sexual and domestic violence is no longer the secret that it was. Although we live in different communities and circumstances, we all share a fear of violence.

We create a false sense of safety when we believe that weapons, locks, dogs and gates make us safe when in reality they can isolate us. In communities where multiple tragedies have taken place, people may think of violence as inevitable and efforts to stop it as futile. But isolation increases vulnerability. Actively facing our own fears so we do not feel vulnerable makes it possible to take action to create safe environments. We become strengthened by joining with others to reduce violence in our communities.

So often it takes a tragedy for communities or neighborhoods to pull together. While effective efforts have been mobilized in response to crises, we don't have to wait for a crisis to take action to create safety nets and prevent violence.

Indeed, personal survival strategies are essential in protecting ourselves, but we must not ignore our power to make change when we take action with others. How much better it would be if what brings us together is the unshakable determination to resist the violence that surrounds us! Breaking down the barriers which divide us to work together is no small task. But the rewards are enormous. It is vitally important for each of us to make community violence prevention part of our personal self-protection strategies.

In this book there are hundreds of ideas for actions to inspire you. We have described people and programs to demonstrate what others have done to prevent violence. There are so many others we have not described, and so many creative ways to get involved. In our twenty-five years of involvement in violence prevention, we have witnessed ordinary people accomplishing the extraordinary: surviving violence, recovering from trauma, answering hotlines, teaching self-defense, educating in neighborhoods and schools, and mobilizing groups to stand up for justice. As parents and, now, grandparents, we have experienced first-hand what it means to be afraid for a child's safety and to desperately wish there were ways to inoculate our children against harm. We are convinced that the only inoculation that exists is personal involvement and collective action. Our hope is that you, like us, will find your own way to get involved.

We have divided this book into three main parts. Part I, JOINING TOGETHER TO PREVENT VIOLENCE, focuses on how to assess the safety of your neighborhood, home and schools, and offers a wide range of strategies for action. While one person on their own can make a heroic effort to stop a mugging or inform police about suspicious actions, the effort is magnified when a group acts together. Just consider the possibilities! The section, OUR NEIGHBORS, offers many actions that might work in your neighborhood. Getting to know your neighbors and your local police can be fun as well as empowering. Have a party, hang out, watch out for one another—people will want to live on your block.

We can't know in advance when violence will occur to ourselves or someone dear to us. But we can make choices and take actions that help us avoid, prevent, resist and survive violence. Talking openly about safety and violence prevention is a necessary first step to keeping our families free from violence. Even young children can be included in safety talks by giving them tools they can use at their age. The section, OUR FAMILIES, gives tips for household safety and techniques for parenting to prevent violence. Parents are alerted to help their children to be media literate and safe in cyberspace.

Whether or not you are a parent, as a community member who is concerned about violence and children, you should become informed about your local school. Safe schools not only offer a good learning environment for children and youth, but also enhance the safety of the community. Communities who care about youth are important in preventing the kind of alienation that leads to youth violence. In the section, OUR SCHOOLS, you will find ways you can participate in teaching children and promoting school policies that keep children safe.

It is amazing how much we can do to keep ourselves from being victimized if we know how. Part II, SAFETY TO GO, contains the nuts and bolts of everyday safety: at work, traveling, at a party or on a date. Do you jog? Do you travel a lot? Have you been thinking about taking a self-defense class? You will find checklists for self-defense classes, car safety and street smarts. Women are more vulnerable to certain kinds of violence, so many of the actions in this section are addressed to women. But men as well as women will find useful suggestions for protecting themselves.

Our newspapers are filled with stories that remind us that violence is a daily concern. In surveys of children and adults, fear about safety and violence rank highest of all their worries. Part III, CONCERNS OF OUR TIMES, addresses the issues that we find most compelling when we look at the complexity of preventing violence in our society. Alcohol and drugs often play a part in acts of violence, adding fuel to the fire. Whether you are a parent wanting to help your children resist alcohol, or whether you are a neighbor wanting to stop drug dealing in your building, the section on ALCOHOL AND DRUGS will help you take action in the best place to start doing something: your own back yard!

Youth-on-youth violence, gang violence and relationship violence are all made more lethal by the fact that young people can so easily obtain guns. Every day, sixteen children are killed by guns in the United States. The strategies in this book to keep kids away from guns and guns away from kids can reverse that trend. So many adults are fearful of teenagers and avoid them. We believe that youth inherited violence, they didn't invent it. As adults, we can become active in their lives, and take responsibility for creating safe environments for them. The section, YOUTH VIOLENCE, suggests ways to teach, mentor, model and give youth the opportunities they need.

Sexual violence is "America's silent epidemic," according to the American Medical Association. Domestic violence is equally serious, sometimes resulting in murder, and causing an intergenerational cycle that perpetuates violence of all kinds. Mistaken beliefs and sexist attitudes continue to be a barrier to stopping sexual harassment, rape and battering. Our section, VIOLENCE AGAINST WOMEN, invites women, men and entire communities to challenge these attitudes and take concrete steps so that women and girls are free from the threat and reality of sexual and domestic violence.

"Racism is the shame of America," said President Bill Clinton in his second inaugural address. While America is a diverse country that values tolerance and freedom, racism, discrimination and hate violence have always been with us. Hate violence is the enactment of hosility towards people's race, gender and sexual orientation. Have you been targeted because you are or appear to be a member of a hated group? For too many of us, this is a familiar experience. You can contribute to turning this around. Become an ally: educate yourself and speak up. The section, HATE VIOLENCE, includes tools to promote tolerance in our communities.

While we emphasize taking action in a personal way, we believe that we also make change by influencing policies and laws that affect us. Don't leave it up to others! In Part IV, we appeal to you to make a personal commitment: Face your fears, find out what is best for your community, become involved and take action. There are MORE than fifty ways to a safer world. Invent your own everyday actions to prevent violence. Make the world safer for us all.

Patricia Occhiuzzo Giggans and Barrie Levy
May 1997

Part I

JOINING TOGETHER TO PREVENT VIOLENCE

OUR NEIGHBORS

DO YOU KNOW . . .

. . . HOW SAFE YOUR NEIGHBORHOOD IS?

Take a few moments to think about your own neighborhood. If you've been reluctant to think about the safety of your streets and parks, remember that knowledge is power. Neighborhoods CAN be made safer through informed action. But first you need the information. Conduct a neighborhood safety audit, asking yourself questions such as the following:

◆ Who uses the local park? Is it safe for children during the day? Is there adult supervision? Is it well lit at night?

◆ Are other public places, such as market parking lots, major streets and alleys, well lit at night?

◆ Do most people walk in your neighborhood, or drive? Are residential streets well lit? Is shrubbery trimmed?

◆ Is there a police or fire station in your neighborhood? How often do the police patrol the area?

◆ Do people in your neighborhood know one another?

◆ What is the incidence of various crimes in your neighborhood? (These statistics are available from your local law enforcement agency.)

◆ Where are the places in your neighborhood where violence is known to occur frequently?

◆ Where does graffiti frequently appear? What has been done to keep the area free of graffiti?

◆ Are there gangs, crack houses or drug dealers in your neighborhood? Are their "turfs" known to community members?

KNOW YOUR NEIGHBORS

Sometimes getting to know your neighbors can be as simple as sitting out in your front yard. Writer Richard Louv and his wife decided to put a wood and metal bench in their front yard. It looked pretty strange and forlorn on their suburban street, but once he and his wife began sitting on their bench, kids and neighbors began to congregate there. Soon the bench became a kind of bus stop that the local kids used for carpools. (Richard Louv, "Renewing Community," *Parents*, January 1996, 40–42.)

Don't have a park bench or a front yard? Here are some other ways to know your neighbors.

1. **Make contact.** Calling on a neighbor in an emergency is much easier to do if you have already established some kind of connection.

   - **Say "hello."** Start simply by saying hello and chatting with the people in your building or on your block. Gradually get to know one another's families and schedules.
   - **Exchange numbers.** Discuss calling upon each other in an emergency of any kind (not just related to violence). Decide what you want neighbors to do if they observe or hear anything suspicious.
   - **Have a party.** Rather than waiting for a crisis to bring you together, find a reason to celebrate and get to know one another while having fun.

2. **Be observant.** Keep your eyes and ears open for unusual incidents, people, noises or violent behavior which might affect you or your neighbors.

A violent mugging occurred across the street from Mindy Lake Einhorn's home in Los Angeles. She canvassed her neighbors and soon had the mugger's license number. She called the police sergeant and gave him the number. Within six hours the mugger was in custody and was later convicted.

3. **Be kid conscious.** If children live nearby, next door or in your building, pay attention to their safety. Inform parents of anything that concerns you. Remember the African proverb, "It takes a village to raise a child." See yourself and your neighbors as a village sharing responsibility for everyone's children.

Deirdre Brooks, Anita Watley and Dorothy Djanie are "block leaders" in Kansas City. Each "neighbors" about 45 children and youth who live nearby and whose families responded to recruitment flyers. They offer homework help, safe houses, field trips, cooking classes, wake-up services, parent education, transportation, school advocacy and snacks.

In Cincinnati, Terrie Walsh's daughter was living with a boyfriend who beat her up. She asked a woman who lived in the next house to call her if she ever saw that her daughter was in trouble. One day, Terrie got a call from the neighbor. "Your daughter's been hurt! Come quick!" That call saved her daughter's life.

4. **Hang out in the 'hood.** In addition to knowing your immediate neighbors, get to know the people and physical environment of your wider neighborhood. Do you know where the nearest emergency room, police station and fire station are? If not, you need to spend more time close to home.

GET INVOLVED

Turn on the six o'clock news and you'll inevitably hear a story of a mugging, a shooting, a rape or some other violent act. What you WON'T hear about is a quiet revolution happening in communities across the country: the grassroots formation of neighborhood groups created to prevent violence and foster caring and community. Neighborhood crime watch groups alone now include some 17 million volunteers in 20,000 communities—almost double the number from a decade ago, according to the National Association of Town Watch.

Neighborhood Watch groups and other community violence prevention coalitions have formed teams that watch for and paint over gang graffiti as soon as it appears. They have successfully deterred gangs from establishing "turf" near their homes or apartments. They have set up safe places for children to go in emergencies, and they have organized marches to raise awareness. By inviting young people and adults to join together to make peace happen in their neighborhoods, these groups work hard to combat the hopeless view that violence is not preventable.

1. **Be a joiner.** There may be a neighborhood association, a tenants' organization or crime watch group already going strong in your community. Talk to neighbors to find out or call your local police precinct's community relations officer.

2. **Be a starter.** To start a neighborhood organization, take the following steps:

- **Talk to neighbors.** Talk to five neighbors about their views on the problem that concerns you.
- **Distribute flyers.** Arrange with other concerned neighbors to hold a meeting in one of your homes. Hand out flyers about the meeting to every unit in your apartment building or every house within a few blocks of yours.
- **Host a meeting.** Facilitate a meeting where all participants discuss problems and brainstorm strategies for addressing them. If you need information, invite a resource person to attend. Define a focus that everyone agrees upon. Develop a plan of action, decide on concrete steps to be taken and arrange for the next meeting.

The Community Organized Protection Plan (COPP) program in Los Angeles started when a neighbor had a meeting in her house after a violent robbery. Forty-five people came. Now they cover 36 blocks with visible volunteer car patrols that report anything suspicious to the police. Since the patrols began, crime has decreased significantly and break-ins have been virtually eliminated in the area.

In Colorado concerned citizens don their roller blades and skate hundreds of miles to fight crime. These intrepid in-line skaters scour bike paths and other public spots from Aurora to Boulder. They're members of RADAC—Residents Against Drugs and Crime—a group that now has over 300 members.

And there's nothing more revitalizing than a neighborhood march and rally. Every August neighborhood groups from Los Angeles to Detroit to Boston band together and take to the streets to participate in the National Night Out Against Crime.

3

PERSONALIZE THE POLICE

With their nightsticks and guns, police officers are intimidating. Yet, the benefits of befriending your local cops are substantial. Just knowing a police officer's name might keep you from being put on hold when you call the local precinct. You are a community member, and police officers are part of your community.

1. **Kibitz with cops.** One friend tells of how she got over her police phobia. Each morning she'd stand in line with two police officers at her local bagel shop. She'd see them joking with the cashier, talking about their families. It suddenly dawned on her, "Hey, these guys are people." One morning before she asked for her poppyseed bagel, she introduced herself and even aired some of her concerns about the neighborhood. Now each time she sees these two on the beat, they wave or even chat with her. And—she feels somehow safer.

2. **Know the PD.** Don't wait for a tragedy or crisis to occur before finding out how your local police department operates. Call the police department's community relations officer. Observe policing patterns in your neighborhood. If you don't see the police at all, or if you see them too much, your community has a problem. Call your police station's watch commander if you have a question or complaint. You might want to ask:

   - Does your neighborhood have community policing?
   - Do police officers patrol on foot, on bike, in the car?
   - Is there a local substation?
   - How many police officers are there in your area and who are they?

- How does a community member go about making an official complaint?

   The COPS (Community Oriented Policing Squad) in New Orleans uses both a tougher and a softer approach to community policing. Tougher means more aggressive intervention. Softer means more neighborhood-friendly tactics, foot patrolling and problem solving. "We do neighborhood clean-ups, counseling on child abuse, you name it," says Officer Djuana Adams. "We help the children with their homework and they show up for treats when they get good grades." The result: Face-to-face contact between police and the people in the community has helped restore trust and reduce crime. (Richard Lacayo, "Law and Order," TIME, January 15, 1996.)

3. **Police the police.** If your community has a history of unfair police practices or incidents of police brutality, join with others to hold them accountable as well as to build positive relationships. After the videotape of Rodney King being beaten by Los Angeles police officers was made public, the LAPD responded by investigating racist police practices.

4. **Be vigilant, not a vigilante.** Some cities and towns have auxiliary police groups, volunteers who assist the police. If you're really gung ho about crime prevention, maybe you can join one of these groups or informally patrol the block yourself. Be careful though—there's a fine line between concerned citizen and vigilante: You don't want to take on something you both shouldn't and can't handle on your own. Always coordinate with or report your efforts to your local police.

   In Venice, California, Ms. Boston Dawna has done night patrols in her neighborhood for two and a half years. Equipped with a flashlight, a cellular phone

and a police scanner, she talks, questions, observes and sometimes catches crooks. Boston Dawna has assisted in more than 100 felony arrests. (K. Chang, "Criminals in Dawna's Neighborhood Better Watch Out," LOS ANGELES TIMES, November 1995.)

5. **Get wired.** More and more citizen watch groups are using state-of-the-art technology to help police the neighborhood. In 11 Miami-area communities, for instance, thefts went down 9% and burglaries fell by one third after citizen watch groups got cellular phones. If you want to be a phone-toting crime stopper, contact your local police department.

Resources

The cellular phone industry is encouraging its members to give away 50,000 cellular phones to neighborhood watch groups around the country. Any watch group can apply with the approval of its local police department. You can get an application by sending email to the Community Policing Consortium in Washington, D.C.: cpc@communitypolicing.org.

OUR FAMILIES

DO YOU KNOW . . .

. . . HOW SAFE YOUR HOME IS?

Think like an intruder. Try to break into your own house or apartment. How easy is it? Here are home safety ideas; add your own.

- Place lights at all entrances and in apartment hallways.
- Use timed lighting on the interior and exterior of your home.
- Install locks on windows and dead bolt locks on doors.
- Use your last name only on the mailbox.
- Place special locks on all sliding doors.
- Install a peephole or a wide angle viewer on the door.
- Avoid indicating you are home alone either on the phone or to someone at the door.
- Record a phone message that doesn't "give away" your absence or schedule.
- Ask for identification of any repair person before opening the door.
- Avoid hiding house keys in any place where they might be found.
- If you lose your keys, have locks changed as soon as possible.
- Clean out shrubbery blocking view of any entrances.
- Install security systems if possible, affordable and feasible.
- If there are guns in your house, get rid of them. Or, if you choose to keep guns, make sure they are unloaded and locked up.

4

DEVELOP A HOUSEHOLD SAFETY PLAN

Come up with a set of specific guidelines to help everyone in the family deal with potential violence—even the youngest and extended family members. Your household safety plan should include discussions of violence prevention as well as instructions for handling disasters such as fires, hurricanes or earthquakes.

1. **Brainstorm.** Over time take the opportunity with household and family members to discuss any and all potential emergencies or incidents of interpersonal violence. No concern should be considered too large or too small. Plan how to respond by looking at various options: who to call, actions to take, guidelines for what to do or not to do. Make sure that the responsibilities fit capabilities. For instance, even young children can be taught how to dial 911.

2. **Post a shortlist.** Make an at-a-glance list of telephone numbers that includes 911, doctors, hospitals, hotlines, and friends and neighbors to call for help, in addition to emergency assistance or violence prevention information. Put the list on bright-colored paper and post it where everyone can find it. Add numbers where parents can be reached if children are at home alone.

3. **Teach and train.** Every member of your household needs to learn how to use the safety plan. Teach them any skills they need in order to implement the plan.

   • How to use the telephone and how to call 911.
   • Self-defense strategies for personal assault situations.

- Assertiveness skills, for example, how to deal with a bully, a sexual harasser or someone who is hostile and aggressive.
- Conflict resolution and negotiation skills.
- First aid and cardiopulmonary resuscitation (CPR).
- Skills for getting to and from school safely, and for being safe when at home alone.
- Teach children to know that their bodies belong to them, how to say no, to get away and to tell a trusted adult if someone tries to touch or hurt them.

5

ALERT KIDS TO THE DANGERS OF STRANGERS

Without scaring children, or turning them into anxious and suspicious people, we need to give them specific guidelines for how adults are supposed to behave towards them, and what to do if an adult does not behave appropriately.

Make sure to teach children that following rules is important, but it is even more important to use their heads and to ask themselves, "What is the safest thing to do in this situation?"

1. **Make stranger dangers clear.** Help kids differentiate between helpful strangers and harmful strangers. A child approaching a stranger for help is generally a safer situation than an adult or older kid approaching a child for help. Asking for help is one way that strangers approach children when they intend to harm them. Adults don't need help from kids to solve their problems.

   - In public places point out or introduce your child to security guards, police officers and others who could help them if they are lost or in danger.
   - Here are some clear ways to tell kids what behavior is OK and what is not OK:

     It's OK for a stranger to say hi and smile, but that's all.

     It's not OK for a stranger to ask you to do something.

     It's not OK for *any* adult to touch you in an inappropriate place.

2. **Give clear DOs and DON'Ts.** Instruct children to tell you or another adult if anyone has frightened them or made them feel uncomfortable. Here are a few examples:

- Don't get into a car with anyone unless it's OK with parents.
- Do stay away from any adult who follows you.
- Do use a buddy system.
- Do ask parents' permission to leave the yard or play area to go into someone's home.
- Do refuse gifts from someone you don't know well.
- Do say no to anyone who wants to take your picture.
- Do say no and leave if someone does anything that makes you uncomfortable.
- Do avoid isolated places.
- Do yell to get attention.

3. **Give age-appropriate instructions.** You're not going to burden kindergartners with a catalogue of all the inappropriate ways that adults can behave. It is only necessary to say, "If a stranger talks to you or does something you don't like, say no and then go tell an adult." Older children, however, can be told that a trustworthy adult would not ask them for directions or that they should be wary of a teen or adult who gives them gifts.

4. **Give kids safe places.** In nearly 100 cities youngsters who feel threatened can go to A Safe Place, a program developed by the YMCA. Participating businesses, fire stations, libraries and other organizations display a yellow-and-black diamond that telegraphs their willingness to take in a frightened child until a parent or other caregiver arrives. Tap into the YMCA's program or start your own. (Laura Sessions Stepp, "Missing Children: The Ultimate Nightmare," *Parents*, April 1994.)

In the neighborhood surrounding the University of Southern California's University Park campus

volunteers in a program called Kid Watch keep their eyes on children as they walk to and from school. Volunteers spend time outdoors from 8:00 a.m. to 9:00 a.m. and from 3:00 p.m. to 4:00 p.m. Additionally there are 63 approved Kid Watch sites—homes where children can go in an emergency. (Marilyn Gardner, "Neighborhood Defense: Watchful Eyes, Caring Hearts," CHRISTIAN SCIENCE MONITOR, October 21, 1996, 10–12.)

Resources

The National Center for Missing and Exploited Children puts out a school curriculum titled "Kids and Company: Together for Safety." The curriculum uses videos, games, puzzles and songs to educate children from kindergarten through the eighth grade. For details call 1-800-843-5678.

6

TEACH SAFETY SMARTS TO KIDS

"At first I froze. Then I thought, I better get outta here. So I climbed out my bedroom window and ran to my neighbor's house and called the police." That's how nine-year-old Jeffrey caught a burglar. Safe kids are safety smart. They trust their instincts, think on their feet and don't hesitate to protect themselves. There are ways parents can raise safety smart children.

1. **Teach your children how to think.** Unexpected situations arise for which rehearsals or rules cannot prepare us. We can prepare our children to meet these challenges by helping them to practice thinking quickly and creatively. Encourage and reinforce independent thinking and problem solving in everyday situations. Value your children's own thoughts and solutions, even when you don't agree with them. Whenever possible in situations requiring decisions, help them to look at options rather than making the choices for them.

2. **Don't teach fear; teach facts and strategies.** Resist transmitting your fear and paranoia to your children. Children can act to maximize their safety when they feel strong, capable and free to think. Be factual and calm when discussing personal safety with children. They need realistic information and tools that are suitable for their age.

3. **Play the "What if" game.** Ask your child what they would do if they encountered potentially dangerous situations. For example, "What would you do if you were walking home from school and someone stopped their car and offered you

baseball cards?" Or, "How would you handle a situation with a big kid who wanted your money?"

- Guide your children through their thought processes. "If you did that, what do you think would happen next?"
- Give them time to think.
- Give positive reinforcement. "What a good idea . . . " Or, "That's a safe thing to do . . . "
- Ask open-ended questions. "How would you feel?" "What do you think . . . ?" "Who would you tell?"
- Emphasize positive steps kids can take to keep themselves safe.

4. **Respect instincts.** Help your child to know that feeling uncomfortable, "icky" or frightened is a sign that something is wrong. Instruct them to see these warning signs as natural tools that can protect them.

5. **Cultivate assertiveness.** Children are safer when they know they have a right to stand up for themselves. Teach your children the difference between passive, aggressive and assertive responses, and that each of these is valuable depending on the situation. For example, with a bully, sometimes it's better to give up your money and walk away (passive response). In some situations, it's better to be ready to fight back to defend yourself, confronting the bully verbally (aggressive). And in other situations, it's better to say no firmly and refuse to comply (assertive).

Resources
"Keeping Kids Safe" is a video from the Personal Safety Series, PSI Productions, P.O. Box 8531, Essex, VT 05451.

PRINCIPLES OF POSITIVE DISCIPLINE

Discipline is a part of child rearing. Its purpose is to set limits and to teach right from wrong. There are no perfect methods of disciplining because every family, every child and every situation is different. What is important is to let your children know that even when they have misbehaved you still love them.

BE PATIENT. Try to be patient, especially when your child doesn't know right from wrong. Ask yourself, "Am I expecting my child to do more than he or she is capable of?"

BE FLEXIBLE. Try different approaches to see what works best for each child, and what works best in different circumstances.

BE FIRM AND FAIR. Be consistent. Make the discipline fit the behavior. Ask yourself, "Did my child misbehave, or am I frustrated from other problems and taking them out on him or her?"

DISCUSS. Discuss your family's rules often so your children know what is expected of them.

SHARE THE RESPONSIBILITY. It is important for both parents and others who are actively involved with your children to agree jointly on discipline, standards and rules.

TIMING. If your child misbehaves, don't wait until you lose your temper to discipline them. If you find anger is taking control, it might help for you and your children to take a time-out.

DO NOT SPANK OR HIT. Think about the long- and short-term effects of spanking. Spanking may teach children to use violence to resolve problems, and siblings to hit one another.

TEACH. Children need to make mistakes in order to learn and grow. Use discipline as a way to teach with your actions as well as your words. Explain so that they understand their misbehavior and the consequences.

SUGGESTED TECHNIQUES FOR POSITIVE DISCIPLINE:

RESTRICTION. Have your child sit in a quiet place for a limited period of time, for example, five minutes.

LOSS OF PRIVILEGE. Take away a privilege, such as watching TV, for a certain amount of time. Be reasonable on your time limits. Do not take away food or meals as a method of punishment.

PRIVILEGES. Offer special privileges for good behavior. By being rewarded for good or appropriate behavior, your children learn that you notice them when they are behaving well, not just when they are disruptive or misbehaving.

(Adapted from "I Want to Be a Good Parent," KCET-TV and Los Angeles Commission on Assaults Against Women, 1988.)

7

PARENTING FOR VIOLENCE PREVENTION

Violent behavior is *learned* behavior. And, unfortunately, it is all too often learned by children at home—from seeing one parent strike or lash out at another, or from being hit or verbally abused themselves. Raising children to be nonviolent, healthy and resilient is not something that parents or caregivers can expect the schools to do alone: It is the responsibility of parents, the extended family and the community.

1. **Be violence free.** Children are more observant and imitative than you may realize.

   - Refrain from using violent words or actions when reacting to conflicts, stress or anger.
   - If you have a problem because of your need to control other people, your own jealousy or your explosive temper, get help. Your behavior frightens your children, and teaches them to abuse others.
   - Use conflict resolution, open communication, listening and assertiveness skills. If these skills are weak, attend workshops, classes or counseling.
   - Develop support systems and positive outlets for dealing with problems or stress.

2. **Discipline with dignity.** Discipline your children by communicating clearly. Set clear expectations and consequences without resorting to physical or verbal abuse. Make an agreement among all family members not to escalate arguments or anger to the point of violence. For example, agree to take

time-outs—stopping the argument for a period of time to allow people to cool off—or agree not to discipline your children when you are too angry to think clearly.

3. **Discuss ethics, values and violence with your children and other members of your household.** The aim is to stimulate thinking, formulate beliefs and develop an awareness of shared family values about violence and its effect on others. Here are several suggested topics for discussion:

- Is violence ever justified?
- Is it ever appropriate to "hit back"?
- What attitude towards violence is reflected in the movie we just saw? Do you agree or disagree?
- What is violence?
- Can words be violent?
- What do you think about owning or using guns?
- Should you get involved if you witness a violent act?
- What causes violence?

> Darlene White, a mother from Lansing, Michigan, is all in favor of family discussion. "I relish the conversations with both my teenagers. We debate about the news and stories on TV and in the movies. It gives me an opportunity to hear what my kids are thinking about and what affects them. I know it pays to talk about these things because recently my 17-year-old son, Alex, stopped hanging out with a friend because he found out that he had a gun. I realize I respect the way my kids think about things, and I know that this is rooted in our family discussions."

4. **Teach empathy.** People who use violence against others do not see the person they are victimizing as a human being with feelings. They do not care what the victim is experiencing or feeling. They lack the capacity for empathy. Prevent violence by teaching children empathy.

- Don't minimize your children's and other people's experiences and feelings.
- Teach your children to imagine other people's experiences and feelings.
- Listen so that you really take in your children's experiences and expressions of feeling.
- Let boys cry and let girls be angry. Let all children feel the full range of emotions.

8

CREATE A PARENTS' SUPPORT NETWORK

Joan felt like her first month as a new mother was a trial by fire: Her premature baby was colicky and breast-feeding around the clock. There were days when the baby just wouldn't stop crying, times when Joan admits she was afraid she would hurt her. Fortunately, she had picked up a flyer advertising a "New Mom Support Group." On one particularly bad morning Joan bundled up her baby, went to the support group and promptly burst into tears. Two hours later, she came away with five phone numbers of other new mothers, a pamphlet on how to help your baby stop crying and a tip on an affordable, reliable baby-sitter.

Whether dealing with a howling newborn or a sullen teenager, parents need to let off steam and connect with other parents. If your community doesn't already have a support network for parents, here's how to weave one:

1. **Be a parent to every kid.** Expand your own idea of parenting to include care and concern for everyone's children. Parents feel less pressure when they know they can rely on neighbors, and children benefit when there are more adults to whom they can turn.

2. **Start parenting support groups.** Create breast-feeding support groups, new mother and father groups, parenting classes, toddler play groups, evening gatherings where parents can let off steam and seek advice. The possibilities are infinite, but the space may be limited. Seek out local

churches and synagogues to see if you can use their space. Most parenting groups ask for a small donation from attendees to cover minimal rent, coffee and refreshments. Publicize the group with flyers that address parents *and* caregivers.

3. **Publish for parents.** Technology has made it easier to quickly put out a professional-looking publication. Get together with other parents to publish a newsletter for parents in the community. The newsletter can feature articles on safety and violence prevention as well as neighborhood activities and organizations.

4. **Push for quality, affordable child care.** Join with others to evaluate child-care needs and resources in your area. Approach local businesses about providing child care for employees. Work with local legislators to increase child-care resources.

5. **Remember: Caregivers are parents, too.** Chances are, if your nanny or baby-sitter is a parent, spending time with your child is taking her away from her own. Be sensitive to caretakers' needs to see their own children or to spend time with a sick child. Encourage friendships between your children and your caregiver's children or grandchildren.

6. **Give future parents a head start.** Introduce special sessions on parenting and child care in elementary grades through high school. Teaching boys and girls about the importance and complexity of child rearing can promote caring and responsible parenting and bring down teen pregnancy rates. From an early age, boys can learn what it means to become an involved and committed father, and girls can learn what it takes to meet the needs and demands of a child.

Resources

For information about starting child-rearing classes in schools, contact Educating Children For Parenting, 2000 Hamilton Street, Suite 206, Philadelphia, PA 19130-3847, (215) 496-9780, educhild@libertynet.org.

WHAT IS CHILD ABUSE?

CHILD ABUSE includes physical abuse, sexual abuse, neglect and emotional maltreatment.

PHYSICAL ABUSE is any act which results in nonaccidental physical injury.

SEXUAL ABUSE is sexual molestation, assault or exploitation of a minor.

NEGLECT is negligent treatment or maltreatment of a child by a parent or caretaker under circumstances indicating harm or threatened harm to the child's health or welfare.

EMOTIONAL MALTREATMENT is emotionally abusive behavior such as verbal assault, unpredictable responses, continual negative moods, constant family discord and double-message communication. It also includes emotional deprivation, that is, the deprivation suffered by children when their parents do not provide the normal experiences producing feelings of being loved, wanted, secure and worthy.

THE FACTS ABOUT CHILD ABUSE

Two million reports of child maltreatment involving 2.9 million children were made in the United States in 1994.

In 80% of reported cases, the abuser is one of the child's natural parents.

The average age of abused children is seven. The average age of abusers is 31.

A 1991 U.S. Justice Department survey of child sexual abusers found that one third of child molesters had attacked their own child or stepchild, and another half had been a friend, acquaintance or more distant relative of the abused child. Only one in seven abusers had molested a child who was a stranger.

(Sources: National Council on Child Abuse and Neglect, "Child Maltreatment, 1994;" Los Angeles Times, January 6, 1996.)

9

PROTECT THE FUTURE: PREVENT CHILD ABUSE

More than three million children are reported as victims of child abuse and neglect each year. Many more do not come to the attention of authorities. Sadly, three children die each day in our country as a result of maltreatment. Children get caught in an intergenerational cycle of violence. If we stop child abuse, we may be able to prevent criminal and abusive adult behavior as well.

1. **See the signs.** The signs of child abuse or neglect are not always so obvious as bruises or burns. If a child you know exhibits one or more of the following signs of abuse, consider making a report to child protective services or police. Report abuse if you have strong evidence or suspicions that a child is being harmed.

   * Signs of nonaccidental injury, such as burns, bruises or welts.
   * Unexplained or repeated bruises or other injuries.
   * Extremes in the child's behavior, such as extreme aggression or extreme withdrawal.
   * Signs of fear, such as fear of parents or other caretakers, or of going home.
   * Explicit knowledge of sexual acts or sexualized behavior inappropriate for the child's age.
   * Sudden changes in the child's behavior, for example, not concentrating in school, or losing interest in friends or activities.

2. **Advocate family services.** Communities need comprehensive services that address issues affecting families. Parenting

programs, health care, housing and employment are vital to maintaining healthy children and families.

3. **Give a parent a break.** Assisting a friend or neighbor with child care or offering to locate sources of community help can provide a welcome boost for someone who is struggling with parenting responsibilities. Your religious and social groups can provide support to families who are members.

4. **Put child abuse prevention on the agenda.** Support and suggest programs on child abuse prevention for local organizations. Civic clubs, the PTA, women's and men's clubs, church groups and schools can offer opportunities for raising public awareness.

5. **Take a child under your wing.** Take part in a mentoring program that gives children and their families an added resource in the form of volunteers who spend time in encouraging and stimulating activities with children.

> **One victim of child abuse cautions, "It shouldn't hurt to be a kid. We must listen to children, protect them and nurture them. I sometimes wonder how different my life would have been if there had been someone in my childhood who was able to hear me, be with me, protect me, someone who could have asked, 'Has someone hurt you?'" (California Office of the Attorney General, CHILD ABUSE PREVENTION HANDBOOK, 1993.)**

Resources

Childhelp USA/Forrester National Child Abuse Hotline, 1-800-4A-CHILD.

National Clearinghouse on Child Abuse and Neglect, 1-800-394-3366.

10

HELP TEENS HAVE HEALTHY RELATIONSHIPS

Help your teens learn the skills and attitudes they need to maintain healthy intimate relationships—not abusive ones. Parents can't eliminate danger, but they can help teens reduce the risks they take. Teaching teens to be aware, alert and assertive gives them the ability to think and take action in all kinds of situations.

1. **Be real.** Talk to your teens about the realities of dating violence:

   - It can happen to anyone.
   - It is serious.
   - Girls stay in violent relationships because they want to be loved or because they are afraid—not because they like or seek abuse.

2. **Encourage assertiveness.** Be wary of labeling female children as pushy or aggressive when they stand up for themselves and their beliefs. Instead, encourage them.

   - Encourage your child or teen to take a self-defense or a public speaking course to develop assertiveness skills and confidence in voicing opinions.
   - Ask your teen, "Have you ever said yes when you wanted to say no?" Discuss and practice what he or she might have said or done if given another chance. The point is for teens to practice articulating effectively what they want or need.

3. **Accentuate the positive.** Open a dialogue to stimulate teens

to think about what qualities to look for in a boyfriend or girlfriend, and what to expect in a healthy relationship. Point out features of healthy relationships when teens see them in real life, books and movies.

4. **Confront your cultural beliefs.** For example, if your religious beliefs require that your daughter must marry her boyfriend "because you've been with him, even if he beats you," then you must challenge yourself to look at your daughter's situation from a perspective of her safety and health.

5. **Name abuse when you see it.** Speak up when you see abuse in relationships, even if those involved are your friends. Silence reinforces the impression among youth that violence in relationships is normal.

6. **Don't put your head in the sand.** Teach your sons and daughters to be responsible about their sexuality. For example, encourage them to make responsible decisions about abstinence, birth control and protection against AIDS and other sexually transmitted diseases. Teach them to distinguish between consensual sex and sexual assault.

Resources
For further information on teen dating violence, see the authors' books, In Love and In Danger: A Teen's Guide to Breaking Free of Abusive Relationships *and* What Parents Need to Know About Dating Violence, *both published by Seal Press (see the back of this book for more information).*

CHARACTERISTICS OF HEALTHY RELATIONSHIPS

Partners share feelings of love, passion, affection, some likes and dislikes, and they enjoy spending time together.

Both partners give and take, each getting his or her way some of the time and compromising some of the time.

They respect each other and value one another's opinions.

They support and encourage one another's goals and ambitions.

They trust one another and learn not to inflict jealous and restrictive feelings on the other if they should arise.

Neither partner is afraid of the other.

They communicate openly and honestly and make each other feel safe to express themselves.

They share responsibility in decision making.

They accept the differences between them.

They encourage each other to have friends and activities outside the relationship.

MONITOR MEDIA MAYHEM

The average child will see 20,000 murders and 80,000 assaults before leaving elementary school. We're not talking about children witnessing violence on the street, but right in the comfort of their living rooms on the television screen.

While the effect of TV violence is widely debated, most people no longer doubt that there is a link between watching violence and committing or permitting violence. The American Psychological Association's Commission on Violence and Youth found that 1) accepting TV violence leads to more aggressive behavior, 2) watching excessive violence leads people to believe the world is more mean and dangerous than it is, 3) a numbness towards violence can result in less likelihood of taking action on behalf of victims and 4) the more violent material viewers see, the more they crave in order to keep stimulated.

In the past few years there has been a grassroots movement not only to monitor media messages but also to respond to and influence them.

1. **Be video vigilant.** While new inventions like the V-chip block violent programming from your TV screen, there is no substitute for the "parent" V-chip. However many programs are blocked, previews for violent shows will still make their way to the screen and kids will still watch TV at their friends' houses. Also, some parents oppose the V-chip as censorship. Be video vigilant and:

- Keep TVs out of kids' bedrooms.
- Set an example by watching nonviolent TV programs.
- Set clear limits on time spent watching TV and content of programs watched.
- Be observant about what your kid is watching.

2. **Nudge the networks.** Does the idea of approaching the networks seem daunting or pointless? Remember that the networks' success depends upon whether we, the consumers, like what we see. If you don't like what you see, make a phone call or write a letter.

> **Diane Levin, a child-development expert, founded Teachers for Resisting Unhealthy Children's Entertainment, or TRUCE, a Somerville, Massachusetts, group of educators and parents. TRUCE members encourage adults to write a letter or make a phone call every week expressing disapproval or approval of what they see in the media, on the Internet and in the marketplace. (CHRISTIAN SCIENCE MONITOR, November 18, 1996.)**

3. **Make kids media literate.** Being media literate means understanding the relationship between TV and advertisers, and that popular culture is not something that happens to us; it's something we create. It means becoming a critical, not a passive, viewer. Get children to challenge what they see and hear, to deconstruct the messages. Ask questions like:

- Who gets hurt?
- Do you think this happens in real life?
- Why do you think the producers picked this kind of music?
- How are men and women portrayed in violent movies or even in violent cartoons?

Discuss alternatives to the violence they see. You can repeatedly assert that no one deserves to be emotionally, verbally or physically abused.

Resources

Center for Media Literacy, 4727 Wilshire Boulevard, Suite 403, Los Angeles, CA 90010, (213) 931-4177, http://www.medialit.org.

Just Think Foundation, 221 Caledonia Street, Sausalito, CA 94965, (415) 289-0122, http://www.justthink.org.

12

CYBERSAFETY FOR CHILDREN

"In allowing our daughter substantial freedom on the Net, we had really been sending her to the candy store with a pocket full of cash and an offhand advisory not to buy anything." G. A. Servi was shocked to find out that her 12-year-old daughter and her friends had been in chat rooms sending messages such as, "Anyone out there want to talk to a hot babe?" and receiving messages back that were sexually explicit. She exerted online parental controls, starting with closing off access to chat rooms. (*Newsweek*, July 3, 1995.)

Abuse involving computers is relatively infrequent. However there are a few risks for children who use online services. Teenagers are more at risk than younger children because they usually use the computer unsupervised, and they are more likely to join in online discussions about relationships or sex. Some risks are:

- **Exposure to inappropriate material.** A child may find sexual or violent material online.
- **Physical molestation.** A child might give information or arrange an encounter with someone online that puts their safety at risk.
- **Harassment.** A child might receive email or bulletin board messages that are harassing, demeaning or hostile.

1. **Get online.** Know how online services work so that you can explain rules for computer use to your children. Learn about

chat rooms, bulletin boards, newsgroups, multi-user games, and other Internet tools. Children learn this technology with ease, so keep up with them and monitor how they are using it.

2. **Supervise.** Assume responsibility for your children's online computer use at home, at school or in the library. Encourage your children to tell you if they encounter messages that are threatening, obscene or make them feel uncomfortable.

3. **Limit access.** Use tools available through Internet providers that allow parents to limit a child's access to online services, blocking out objectionable material, such as adult-oriented chat rooms and bulletin boards.

4. **Make cybersafety rules.** Provide guidance to your children by establishing family rules and guidelines. Here are some DOs and DON'Ts for children:

   • Don't give out identifying information, such as your address or phone number.
   • Don't arrange a face-to-face meeting with someone via the computer without parental permission.
   • Don't respond to messages that are suggestive, obscene, threatening or make you feel uncomfortable.
   • Don't send pictures or anything else without checking with parents.
   • Do remember that people online may not be who they say they are.
   • Do remember that everything you read online may not be true.
   • Do talk with one another about your online experiences.

5. **Check cybersafety at school.** Make sure that your children's schools have standards for conduct when students use classroom computers. School administrators are developing Internet Acceptable-Use Policies (AUPs) so students know what to expect when they go online and what behavior is expected of them.

OUR SCHOOLS

DO YOU KNOW . . .

. . . THE STATS ON VIOLENCE IN OUR SCHOOLS?

- An estimated 20% of all injuries to children and youth occur in and around schools.

- Assaults are the third largest cause of injury in schools, after falls and sports injuries. Assaults include beatings (54%), gunshot wounds (14%), falls from pushing or shoving (11%), stabbings (9%) and being struck by a blunt object (8%).

- The majority of assaults (47%) occur to youth ages 10 to 14; 18% of those assaulted were five to nine years of age.

- School crimes have grown more violent, and perpetrators younger.

- 270,000 guns go to school every day in the United States.

- An estimated 9% of eighth graders carry a gun, knife or club at least once a month.

(Sources: National Pediatric Trauma Registry, October 1988–April 1993; U.S. News and World Report, November 8, 1993.)

13

CONDUCT A SCHOOL SAFETY AUDIT

Here's a pop quiz about your local school: What emergency plans are in place in the event of a violent incident? Is anyone supervising hallways between classes or while children are at lunch? Is there graffiti in the bathrooms, or anywhere else on the grounds? If so, what does it say?

Don't be surprised if you failed the quiz. Most people walk by their community schools each day without a clue as to what goes on inside. And parents may get only a glimpse of a few select areas: the front office, the infirmary, the auditorium or classrooms all decked out for back-to-school night.

A school is often the hub of a community; if the school is not safe and secure, the community isn't either. So if you really want to protect the most valuable treasure of the community, its children, do the rounds of the school grounds.

1. **Do the grand tour.** Walk around the school campus, both inside and out, and the surrounding area. Look for the following:

    *   Safe "corridors" en route to school so that children will not be harassed by drug dealers or walk through unsafe areas.
    *   Safety patrols at bus stops and along the way to school.
    *   Adequate perimeter security, for example, fencing and posted signs with rules.

- Alarms and lights where needed.
- Security patrol or others closely monitoring the grounds and surrounding area.
- Graffiti-free walls.
- A campus that is clean, attractive and in good repair.
- Limited access to people who should not be on campus.

2. **Go to the top.** Because school policies and practices can either prevent or promote violence, set up a meeting with the principal to find out about the following:

- Active involvement of students in violence and crime prevention.
- Emergency procedures for incidents such as fire, accidents or violence.
- Policy for handling intruders, loiterers or nonstudents on campus.
- Policy for dealing with dating violence, sexual harassment and assault.
- Supervision in hallways, corridors and other congregating places for students before and after school, between classes and at lunch.
- Job descriptions for school personnel that include violence and vandalism prevention duties.

3. **Draw up a trouble-shooting plan.** After you complete your audit, list all the things that need to be changed. Work with other parents and concerned citizens to draft a letter to the principal, voicing your opinions. Try to use the letter to arrange a meeting with the principal, teachers and students.

> **Concerned parents at Santa Monica Elementary School in Hollywood, California, evaluated children's safety on the way to school. The result was a plan to create safe corridors to and from the school. Routes to school were monitored by parents, local police and school security guards before and after school. One parent, Linda Perez, claims, "We found that fights,**

bullies harassing younger children and violence around the school area went down. The best thing was that the children felt safer, and so did the parents."

REVIEW SCHOOL RULES AND TOOLS

Is your school a ZTZ? That's short for a Zero Tolerance Zone for violence. Schools across the country are carving out their territory as zero tolerance zones. This standard, emphasized by the principal and entire staff, sets the tone of the school. ZTZ directs policies and procedures for student conflicts, student conduct and schoolwide rules and establishes reasonable consequences for violation of rules. Parents and students even sign forms agreeing to the school's policies.

If the schools in your community aren't ZTZs, then what are their policies? *Everyone* should know about school violence prevention policies, and everyone—students, parents, school staff and faculty and community members—should participate in the development of the policies.

1. **Check your school out.** Here's what ZTZ schools offer:

   ✓ School conduct and discipline code regarding violence, drugs, alcohol and vandalism.
   ✓ Incident reporting system.
   ✓ Sexual harassment and relationship violence policies, covering definitions, procedures for complaints and investigations and consequences of harassing and battering behavior.
   ✓ Rules and consequences regarding guns and weapons on campus.

✓ Effective liaison with local law enforcement.
✓ Training for teachers, administrators and other school personnel, and their active participation in school violence prevention efforts.
✓ Access to trained violence prevention professionals to work with the school when needed, for example, violence prevention education specialists and trauma teams.
✓ Specific policies regarding gang-related activities on campus, for example, prohibiting gang dress, graffiti, hostile behavior and turf battles on campus.

2. **Get with the program.** Support violence prevention seminars in schools in your community. Schools usually have programs that build fundamental skills, such as self-esteem, respect or teamwork skills. Push the school to add programs that respond to current demands on children and youth, such as:

- Dating violence, acquaintance rape and sexual assault prevention.
- Sexual harassment prevention.
- Gang violence prevention.
- Substance abuse prevention.
- School drop-out prevention.
- Truancy prevention.
- Teen pregnancy and AIDS prevention.
- Respect for diversity programs.

   Melissa Caudle, principal of John Martyn High School in Jefferson, Louisiana, said her school's most effective rules governed dress code and contraband items—no book bags, no gang colors or bandanas, no beepers or portable phones, no radios. Parents and students are told that any item worn or brought to school that violates school policy will be confiscated and not returned; both parents and students sign an agreement to this. (Melissa Caudle, "Eight Ways to Safer Schools," THE HIGH SCHOOL MAGAZINE, September 1994, 10–13.)

Wilson Senior High School, in El Sereno, California, trained the entire student body of 2,500, faculty, administrators and all school personnel in a sexual harassment project called "Off Limits." The aim was to make the campus a sexual harassment-free zone. They established adult Complaint Managers for informal resolution of sexual harassment incidents, including determining consequences for harassers. The process provided validation and support for people who had been harassed. The project was sponsored by the Los Angeles Unified School District Gender Equity Commission.

Resources

A videocassette series, "Cooling a Hot Situation," is available free from Health and Safety Education, Area 2-C, Metropolitan Life Insurance Co., One Madison Avenue, New York, NY 10010. The "Hot Situation" tapes are geared towards 7- to 10-year-olds and 11- to 14-year-olds. A video for adults, "Working Together to Prevent Violence," looks at a model program on nonviolence in Kansas City, Missouri.

15

GO BACK TO SCHOOL

A school that is isolated from its community is an impoverished place. When parents, business people and community members get involved in their local school, they not only enrich children's lives—and their own—they create a safety net for the neighborhood children. There will be fewer people who are strangers to be feared, and more people who are acquaintances and friends to whom children can turn for help. Also, as children get to know more adults in the community, they can gain valuable role models.

So, go back to school for an hour a week or even once a month and:

1. **Share your knowledge.**

   - Help with classroom instruction. Be a tutor. Plant a garden. Coach athletics. Assist in the library or the office.
   - Share your cultural history and customs. Expose students to the arts or to various professions and occupations.
   - Offer special seminars for students on subjects like ceramics or public speaking.

     Ms. Tremaine, a sixth-grade teacher in Atlanta has a Career Day in her class every month. Parents of students are invited to describe their careers. The parents represent a broad variety of occupations, such as managers, journalists, domestic workers and full-time homemakers.

2. **Lend a hand—or many.** Organize a graffiti clean-up at your

neighborhood school. Invite local businesses to donate paint and equipment and invite students to participate in cleaning up their school.

3. **Make your business school-friendly.** Suggest that your business donate equipment and expertise to local schools or give workers time off to work in schools. A program called "Alive" in Long Beach, California, arranges for employees in local companies to take time off to be tutors, field trip leaders and to teach violence prevention workshops in schools.

4. **Show someone the ropes.** Or even jump rope with her! Become a mentor or a "big brother" or "big sister."

   - Join an organization that matches young people with adults to spend time doing recreational or educational activities together. Some school districts have mentor programs.
   - You can informally spend time with kids in your neighborhood. For example, you might play pick-up basketball games with kids at the local park or encourage your own child's friends to hang out at your house.

   All of the families on Elizabeth Biggs's block in Broken Arrow, Oklahoma, pitched in to buy a basketball net to put at the end of their cul-de-sac. Impromptu games were soon being played there, drawing everyone outside, either to play or to visit. (Richard Louv, "Renewing Community," PARENTS, January 1996, 40–42.)

   San Diego Unified School District has a graffiti-removal team that works 24 hours a day to immediately remove any gang symbols or fix vandalism that may affect the school's positive image.

16

MAKE AFTER-SCHOOL COOL

Imagine kids wanting to stay at school *after* classes are over, or wanting to go back on a Saturday or Sunday. Here's what it might be like if your local school was a hub of activity, from early morning until evening, weekdays and weekends. Imagine a school where . . .

Rotary Club members come to the campus almost daily to serve as sports coaches, homework tutors and field trip leaders. Retired teachers return to the classroom to offer tutoring. Under the supervision of workers from the city's Parks and Recreation Department, youths play in the schoolyard until the sun sets. The YWCA runs a daycare center for very young children. Children and their families have access to regular medical and dental care and counseling from pro bono practitioners. A medical van from a health clinic visits the campus each week. English classes are available for adults. Arts and crafts classes are available to students in an after-school program.

This is not a dream; it's a description of the after-school refuge provided by Covina Elementary School in Covina, California. The school started 17 programs with the involvement of 19 community organizations. Here are some steps for turning your school into a bustling community center:

1. **Organize.** Discuss your ideas with parents, neighbors, teachers and kids. Create an informal committee. Once projects

have titles and committees to work on them, they become more possible.

2. **Plan.** Meet to discuss the kinds of activities and services that would best respond to the needs of your school, your community and its families. Start small, with just a few activities.

3. **Write a proposal.** Before you put your plans into a proposal, it might be best to look at what other communities have done. Perhaps there is a standard proposal you can use so that you don't have to re-invent the wheel. Don't forget to spell out what programs will cost.

4. **Set up a meeting.** Send your proposal to appropriate school administrators, school board members, community leaders or business people—anyone who has a say in getting your program off the ground or who can invest money in it. Suggest a meeting and do some rigorous follow-up by phone to pin people down and get them to commit to a time.

> **What is the payoff for turning a school into a refuge? At Covina Elementary School the principal and teachers soon noticed that vandalism and gang recruitment on campus had decreased significantly. In addition, community involvement spread to concern about apartment buildings near the school in which drugs and crime were rampant. The city helped organize a neighborhood preservation committee. As a result city code enforcers ordered landlords to improve their buildings and evict the drug dealers. Police stepped up patrols. All of these activities have not only improved the lives of the students and provided resources for their families, but have also created a safer neighborhood. (P. Johnson, "After-School Refuge," LOS ANGELES TIMES, November 22, 1995.)**

17

ENSURE SAFE PLAY SPACES FOR KIDS

When the school day ends—and when school is out for the summer—children and youth spend a good deal of time in local parks and playgrounds. Yet, as city park and recreation budgets have shrunk, these play spaces have fallen into disrepair. Parks have become magnets for the homeless as well as criminals. Many are littered with drug equipment and have become the settings for violent incidents.

Communities must provide safe and encouraging environments for kids to congregate and play. Not only do kids get valuable physical exercise through play, but they also learn to be sociable community members. Safe space can also prevent children from seeking antisocial means to feel safe, such as joining a gang or getting a gun.

1. **Conduct a safety audit.** Remember the school safety audit in action #13? Conduct the same kind of inventory of local playgrounds and parks. You might want to check:

    ✓ Is the area well lit?
    ✓ If there are bathrooms, are they well lit and maintained?
    ✓ Is the playground equipment maintained?
    ✓ Is there graffiti on playground walls or equipment?
    ✓ Are there trash receptacles?
    ✓ Is the playground littered with drug paraphernalia, alcohol bottles or other signs of misuse?

50 Ways to a Safer World

2. **Schedule a meeting.** As taxpayers, community members have the right to demand that playgrounds be properly maintained and staffed and that they offer a full schedule of activities. Arrange a meeting through local community groups or churches to gain support for your cause.

3. **Lobby.** Once your group has identified the government body that can make a difference, such as the parks and recreations commissions, have someone in your group attend civic meetings regularly. Lobby local politicians and police, applying consistent pressure to make your case for safer parks and playgrounds. Get publicity in local media with a few well-placed calls and letters.

4. **And go private.** If you can't effect changes through lobbying local government, go private. Raise funds and involve community members in developing programs that offer supervised activities at recreation or community centers, malls or other gathering places. Collaborate with YWCAs, YMCAs, Boys and Girls Clubs and other youth organizations to develop accessible recreational, educational and tutoring programs for neighborhood kids.

> In the Westlake area of Los Angeles, the neighborhood group More Advocates for Safe Homes created an opportunity for residents to grow their own food and help the community. A vacant lot that was a haven for crime was fenced off to make way for a flower, vegetable and fruit garden. Neighborhood youth were given plots to plant, and a group of youngsters worked on a mural.
>
> In the mid-1980s the GreenSpace Alliance of Boston brought together a coalition of businesses, environmentalists, civic organizations and low-income residents who lived near problem parks in Boston. The group attended city council and state legislative meetings, got the media's attention and finally got

local politicians to listen. Three years after their crusade began, Boston's "tot lots" underwent massive renovation. (Janet Clayton, "Making Playgrounds Safer," ESSENCE, January 1989, 97.)

After a 10-year-old boy was hit by a car while playing in the street in downtown Detroit, neighbors and kids organized a rally and fund drive to clear out a vacant lot to make room for a playground. A local youth club responded by offering to build the playground and sponsor after-school activities.

Part II

SAFETY TO GO

DO YOU KNOW . . .

. . . THE PRINCIPLES OF SELF-DEFENSE?

◆ No one *invites* or *deserves* to be raped, assaulted or abused.

◆ Self-defense strategies emphasize options, choices and risks in taking action to prevent violence or deal with a violent situation.

◆ Fighting back to defend yourself is an option, not an obligation.

◆ Commitment counts. If you decide to use physical self-defense in a situation, commit to the defense and put everything into it.

◆ Spirit first, technique second. Your attitude in taking a stand against an assault is more important than the particular techniques you use.

◆ Your brain and your voice are your best self-defense weapons.

◆ Remember to breathe. Threatening situations stimulate your adrenaline; remembering to breathe relaxes you and enables you to think through the panic.

◆ Effective self-defense uses strength against weakness (your strengths against an attacker's weaknesses), and hard against soft (your muscles against an attacker's vulnerable body parts).

◆ Your goals are to prevent, avoid, resist, escape and survive violence.

◆ In a fight to defend yourself, there are no rules (you do what you must to survive) and there are no guarantees (outcomes are unpredictable).

(Sources: Los Angeles Commission On Assaults Against Women, Women's Self-Defense: A Complete Guide to Assault Prevention, 1987.)

18

TAKE CHARGE OF DEFENDING YOURSELF

While the best way to learn self-defense techniques is to take a class, there are things you can do right now that will increase your chances of surviving a violent incident. Even the way you carry yourself or use eye contact when you're in transit can deter a potential assault.

1. **Empower yourself.** The most basic fact about self-defense is that you do have the power to outwit or outmaneuver an assailant, but you must believe this and convey this to a potential attacker. *Being aware and assertive are fundamental to self-protection.*

   People have been remarkably resourceful in thwarting an attack without ever throwing a punch. When you believe in your own power, you can think quickly and assess your options. In a threatening situation, you might choose to fight back, or you might decide that physical resistance is not in your best interest. The important thing is to know how to defend yourself so that you have choices. This is empowering.

   The purpose of using self-defense techniques is to de-escalate the attack or incapacitate the attacker. The goal is to get away as quickly and safely as possible.

2. **Rely on your natural weapons.** You're already carrying more powerful weapons than pepper spray, mace or an umbrella with a metal point. These are:

   ▪ **Your body.** It contains *many* weapons, such as your fists, your legs and leverage. Your body can communicate assertiveness, resistance to vulnerability and power.

- **Your mind.** It contains the capacity to out-think your assailant, to strategize and to be aware and knowledgeable about what is necessary in order to be safe.
- **Your voice.** It enables you to protect yourself verbally and to utilize a self-defense yell to attract attention, to surprise the assailant and to focus your own power and energy.

3. **Attack vulnerable targets.** If you choose to fight back, you need to respond to the attack with a serious intention to injure. Your aim is to incapacitate the assailant so that you can get away. The five most vulnerable, easily accessible targets on the body are:

- **Eyes.** Eyes are sensitive and therefore a useful target when the attacker is close to you, or pinning you down. Using both thumbs or fingers to press on the eyes will cause pain and temporarily impair vision so that you can escape.

- **Nose.** The nose is fragile, highly visible and easily broken or dislocated. A sharp blow to the nose causes a flow of tears, intense pain and bleeding, which distract an attacker.

- **Throat.** You don't have to use much force to bruise or break a windpipe. Your target is the Adam's apple.

- **Testicles and groin.** The effect of a strike, kick or grab to this area can range from distraction to severe pain and temporary incapacitation. Some male attackers instinctively guard this area, but even if you are not able to "go for the groin" immediately, you can distract your attacker by striking elsewhere first, then go for it.

   Sandy Locke, of Dallas, Texas, reports, "A guy followed me up the stairs to my apartment. As I swung around abruptly and confronted him with a loud yell—

'Get away from me!'—I knocked him down. He fell down the stairs behind him, and I was safe."

Resources

Women's Self-Defense: A Complete Guide to Assault Prevention *is available from the Los Angeles Commission on Assaults Against Women, 6043 Hollywood Boulevard, Suite 200, Los Angeles, CA 90028, (213) 462-1281.*

19

TAKE A SELF-DEFENSE CLASS

Participation in self-defense classes encourages you to think in terms of options and choices, develops your awareness and assertiveness skills and provides practice for physical self-defense techniques. A good self-defense class will expand the way you think about violence prevention, help you deal with your fears and enable you to feel more empowered in your life.

1. **For Women Only.** Let's face it—women are more vulnerable to sexual assault and are more likely to sign up for self-defense classes. If you are a woman, you may be interested in training that is aimed specifically at women.

   Most of the these programs are available through rape crisis centers, YWCAs, women's centers on college campuses and women's martial art schools. Here's what the best women's self-defense training offers:

   - Awareness, safety strategies, assertiveness skills and physical self-defense techniques.
   - Awareness of specific vulnerabilities and issues of women and girls.
   - Classes taught and designed by women with women's experiences, strengths and capabilities in mind.
   - A focus on sexual assault, domestic violence and child abuse prevention.

2. **Size up before you sign up.** In selecting a self-defense course, observe a class or at least talk to the instructor about the philosophy of the class. You can also talk to students in

the class or someone who has taken the course. Keep in mind that a self-defense class is not the same as a martial arts course, though some of the skills taught may be derived from the martial arts. Evaluate a prospective course using the following criteria:

✓ Is the instructor respectful and encouraging? Does she or he respect the experiences and fears that women, in particular, have about violence?
✓ Does the class emphasize rape prevention, including potential assaults by dates and acquaintances as well as assaults by strangers?
✓ Is assertiveness training stressed as an important part of the class?
✓ Are the physical techniques simple and easy to remember?
✓ Is the instructor mindful of the safety of the participants?
✓ Is care taken to allow class members the option of not participating in any practices or role plays that may re-stimulate trauma or fear?

Self-defense classes propose a unique paradox: Students hope they never have to use the techniques they learn in class. April Werner, of Las Vegas, New Mexico, suddenly found herself in a situation in which she had to use what she learned in her self-defense training. Asleep in her dorm room, she was awakened by a man trying to pin her down. She had been disabled with rheumatoid arthritis for years and didn't have the strength to push him off. So April took a deep breath and yelled so loud it was a roar. The assailant ran. Her positive identification of him led to his arrest.

20

BE SOCIAL—SAFELY

Most sexual violence is committed by people known to the victim, but strangers become acquaintances quickly in social situations. When we know a person—however superficially—we may act counter to our instincts, or let our guard down. In a social situation with other people around, don't make the assumption that nothing can happen to you.

Unfortunately for women, with the prevalence of dating violence and date rape, prepping for a party or date involves more than choosing a new outfit or doing your hair. You need to be aware of the potential risks of each social situation.

1. **Plan for safety.** Take precautions and plan for new and different social situations.

   - **Keep a cash stash.** When you go out, have cash and coins for public phones.
   - **Phone home.** Take phone numbers for emergencies. Also, make sure someone knows where you're going and what time you expect to be home.
   - **Designate a driver.** If you are going in a group, choose someone to stay sober and drive everyone home safely.
   - **Chart an escape route.** Plan how to get home if you find yourself in an uncomfortable or threatening situation.
   - **Go public.** Always meet someone you haven't dated before in a public place rather than at your home.
   - **Know your limits.** Do you get a buzz after a white wine spritzer, or can you drink a couple of beers and still feel as solid and levelheaded as always? Be aware of your alcohol

tolerance since many sexual assaults occur when alcohol is used by victim and/or perpetrator.

2. **Be assertive.** Even with all your planning, you may find yourself in an uncomfortable situation. If you do, remember that you CAN take control.

- **Just say no.** Resist the pressure to drink excessively and use drugs at a party or on a date. It is much easier to be in control if you are not under the influence. Be aware of how much your date drinks too. Also, be aware that drugs and alcohol are sometimes used deliberately to incapacitate rape victims. Some of the drugs used are legal, such as Rohypnol, called the "date rape" drug because it induces amnesia.
- **Set clear sexual limits.** If you are pressured to have sex or engage in certain sexual acts when you don't want to, be firm in your refusal.
- **Be independent.** Don't let your date make all the decisions about where you go, and don't rely on him for transportation.

Julie, a 26-year-old from Minneapolis, tells of a near-miss situation that occurred when she met a man at a party: "The fact that he kept insisting on refilling my drink alerted me to be careful and aware. I stayed sober, and insisted on driving home. My friend told me the next day that he has taken girls out, gotten them drunk and forced them to have sex in his car."

21

PREVENT CAR CRIME

Once you're speeding along the highway encased in your chrome-and-steel car with the doors locked and the radio blasting, you may feel invulnerable to crime—safe. Yet violent car crimes, not just theft, have escalated in recent years. Your car can become a moving target in a drive-by shooting, a "smash-and-grab" (in which someone throws something to break your window and then steals your purse) or a carjacking.

Here are some ways to keep from becoming a car crime statistic.

1. **Keep your car fit.** When you keep your car in good shape, you minimize the risk of a breakdown. Also, check your gas gauge frequently; always keep at least a quarter of a tank.

2. **Stock your glove compartment.** Keep the following safety items in your car:

   - flashlight
   - Call Police sign
   - flares
   - cellular phone
   - comfortable shoes
   - street maps
   - pad of paper and pen
   - first-aid kit

3. **Lock criminals out—or track them down.** Consider using a steering wheel locking device and/or an alarm with a fuel or ignition cut-off switch. Tracking systems that enable the

police to locate a vehicle are expensive, but they are effective.

4. **Be aware**. Make awareness and caution a habit.

- Have keys ready when walking to your car.
- Look inside and around your car before entering.
- Enter quickly and lock doors.
- Park in well-lit areas and always lock the car when you leave it.
- Refrain from using an automatic door opener from too far away—all doors will open.
- Don't open your window for suspicious looking people.
- Make sure that a friend is safely inside her home or that her car has started before driving away. Ask friends to do the same for you.

22

USE YOUR CAR FOR SELF-DEFENSE

Your car can be an asset in a threatening situation. When a car crime happens or your car breaks down, consider your options.

1. **Stay in your car.** If your car breaks down, use your emergency flasher. Lift the hood or place a Call Police sign in the window. Stay in your car with the doors and windows locked until the police or a tow truck arrives. If someone stops to help, stay in the car and ask them to call the police. Roll down the window, if you must, only enough to be heard. If you are deaf or hard of hearing, write a note to ask for assistance and hold it against the window.

2. **Find a safe haven.** If you are followed while driving, drive to the nearest police station, fire station or hospital emergency entrance, or go to an open gas station and call the police. If this is not possible, honk your horn and turn on your emergency flashers. Do not pull over on the street or drive directly home if you can avoid it.

3. **Give up your car.** In case of carjacking, or an attempt to steal your car while you are in it, consider giving up your car to protect yourself. If you have a clear escape route, consider driving away. If someone forces their way into your car, attempt an escape as soon as possible, for example, jump out at a red light and run.

4. **Don't make a bad scene worse.** In case of harassment while driving—for example, if someone is making gestures or driving with hostility—refrain from escalating the situation by yelling, swearing or returning the gesture.

5. **Use your car as a weapon of opportunity.** Your car is not just a weapon that can be turned against you.

- You can use your car to escape, or to knock over someone who is threatening you.
- You can use the car door to slam someone.
- You can use your horn to attract attention.
- You can flash your lights to alert someone that you are being followed.
- You can use electric windows to stop someone from reaching in.
- You can crash the car or cause an accident (in a way that does not cause you injury) if you are forced to drive an attacker somewhere; then you can get out and escape.

In a downtown St. Louis shopping center parking lot, a man came up to Monica Gentry's car and menacingly told her to get out and give him the keys. Monica moved quickly and opened the door, slamming it into the man, and knocking the wind out of him. She ran to the nearest store for help.

23

TRAVELING SAFELY—IN TOWN AND OUT

When you leave the driving to others, you don't have to worry about navigating traffic. But it is important to remain alert and aware. Use your safety sense on the road, on the rails and in the air.

1. **Prepare.** Before you leave home, whether to go to work or to take a vacation, take precautions to maximize your safety.

   - Plan your route and itinerary so that you know what to expect.
   - Plan in advance so that you can keep a hand free when carrying luggage or packages.
   - Keep valuables close to your body and secure.
   - In preparation for travel, stop newspaper and mail delivery, or arrange to have them picked up daily. Alert neighbors to your travel plans. Consider installing timers on lights.
   - When traveling to new, unfamiliar places, prepare to reduce your vulnerability by gathering information about transportation from the airport or bus station, travel times between locations, general directions and key landmarks. Get a map.
   - Familiarize yourself with local customs, including standards of dress, to be less noticeable.
   - Whenever possible, make sure someone else has your itinerary (locations, dates, times, telephone numbers, contacts). Let someone know when you have arrived at your destination.

2. **Pay attention.** Be attentive to what is going on around you when using public transportation.

- Refrain from taking naps on bus benches, in trains or in cabs.
- If you begin to feel uncomfortable when making conversation with others, follow your instincts, and end the conversation or move.
- If someone is rubbing against you or touching you inappropriately, be assertive and bring attention to the situation by responding in a calm, but loud and confident voice, "Stop touching me!"
- If someone is harassing you on any form of transportation, take action by alerting the conductor, flight attendant or security person, and moving to another seat or area.
- If you feel someone is following you when you get off the bus, plane or train, walk to a populated area and seek assistance.

3. **Tips for travel.** Cut down on the risks involved in traveling to unfamiliar places by following some simple safety procedures. Be aware that a long airplane flight, jet lag, sleep deprivation and a strange environment can disorient you and make you more vulnerable to victimization.

- **Use luggage that you can handle easily.** Carry valuables, such as money belts, in hidden places or use fanny packs to keep valuables close to your body.
- **Don't draw attention to yourself** by displaying cash or expensive jewelry.
- **Take along safety gadgets,** such as an alarm for hotel room doors or portable travel locks.
- **Choose a safe hotel** that has 24-hour staffing, electronic door keys, dead bolt locks and peepholes in the doors. Leave the Do Not Disturb sign on the door when you are not there, except when you need the room cleaned.
- **Find out about travel advisories** from the U.S. Government regarding safety when traveling outside the United States.
- **Don't look like a tourist.** If you want to read a map, go into a restaurant or coffee shop. Don't stand on a corner

doing it. It is a dead giveaway that you are new in town and don't know where you are.

- **Use recommended tour guides or escorts,** or check their references.
- **Know where to find help.** Locate the nearest police department and know how to contact the embassy or consulate.

24

STREET SMART SAFETY

Attackers look for easy targets, so make it hard for them. Stay alert and aware. Use your body language to convey an "I am not a victim" attitude. Walk with confidence. Look around you. Act as if you belong wherever you are.

1. **Think of safety when you dress.**

   - Wear clothes that do not restrict movement.
   - Wear running shoes and change into dress shoes when you arrive at your destination.
   - Use purses or bags that allow you to keep one hand free.

2. **Buddy up.**

   - Take walks or runs with friends or neighbors.
   - A dog is a good running companion.
   - Avoid being on the street alone if you are upset or under the influence of alcohol or drugs.
   - If you walk or jog alone, whenever possible, take a route where there are other people. Avoid isolated areas or places where attackers can easily hide.

3. **If you are followed:**

   - If you are followed by someone on foot, check over your shoulder, then cross the street and walk in the other direction.
   - If you are followed by someone in a car, turn around and walk in the opposite direction. Try to get a description of the car and the license number.
   - If you continue to be followed, walk towards people. Seek assistance.

4. **If you are in trouble:**

   - Do not hesitate to get attention however you can.
   - Do not be afraid to make a scene.
   - Ignore verbal attacks or verbal harassment. Keep moving.

5. **Elevators.** When using elevators, follow your instincts. If you are uncomfortable getting on, wait for the next one. If you are already on and become uncomfortable, get off at the next floor and wait for another one. If you are threatened while on an elevator use the alarm to get attention.

6. **ATMs.** When using ATMs, pay attention. Watch for people hanging around. Prepare your transaction in advance and conduct your business quickly. Avoid using isolated ATMs.

25

SAFETY AT WORK

Dave was under a lot of stress at home and at work, and his coworker Steve worried about him. Steve was promoted and Dave was not. Soon Steve noticed that Dave was increasingly moody, picking fights and threatening coworkers. Steve used his company's anonymous alertline run by their Employee Assistance Program to report his concern. A manager worked with the EAP to help Dave deal with his problems, and potential violence was avoided.

The workplace is not immune to the hazards and terrors of interpersonal violence. According to the United States Department of Labor Relations, one out of every six violent crimes occurs at work. Threats, pushing, shoving and fist fights are the most common, and there are increasing numbers of reports of sexual harassment.

1. **Pay attention.** If you notice that a coworker is stressed, disgruntled and exhibiting signs of aggression, tell a manager or someone who can find out what's going on and help.

2. **Advocate for safety planning in your workplace.** With your coworkers and managers, advocate for well-defined company policies and training to prevent violence, such as:

   - Hiring procedures that adequately screen applicants.
   - Help for dismissed employees to deal with stress.
   - Crisis plans for what to do in a potentially violent situation.
   - Mechanisms for lodging complaints against sexual or other kinds of harassment.

- Personal safety and self-defense training.
- Policies to address safety of battered women employees.
- Prohibitions against guns and other weapons at work.

3. **Practice positive management.** Be proactive in dealing with employee problems. Train your supervisors and employees to practice violence prevention management.

- Intervene early when trouble surfaces.
- Detect warning signs of potential violence.
- Document threatening actions in reports.
- Report threats to management and security.
- Refer troubled employees for counseling.

4. **Assess the safety of your workplace environment.** Assess and make safe all buildings and facilities, indoors and outdoors, such as exits, parking and lighting. For example, provide appropriate lighting and escort services for employees, or install panic or alert buttons in customer service areas.

Resources

"Preventing Violence in the Workplace Resource Guide," 1995, by the United Way Los Angeles and the Violence Prevention Coalition of Greater Los Angeles is distributed by United Way Planning and Community Services, 523 West Sixth Street, Los Angeles, CA 90014.

Part III

CONCERNS OF OUR TIMES

ALCOHOL AND DRUGS

DO YOU KNOW . . .

... THE LINK BETWEEN ALCOHOL AND DRUGS AND VIOLENCE?

◆ Studies have found that 50–60% of homicide and serious assault offenders were drinking when they committed the offense.

◆ Over 70% of incarcerated individuals were convicted of crimes that related in some way to alcohol and drugs.

◆ A study of alcohol availability in Santa Clara County, California, found that those census tracts with the highest concentration of outlets which sell alcohol also reported the highest numbers of crimes and requests for police services.

◆ Alcohol and drugs are present in a substantial number of sexual assault and domestic violence incidents. Drug abuse is connected to large numbers of robberies, committed to support drug "habits."

◆ It is projected that a 10% increase in alcohol consumption will lead to a 6.7% increase in rape, a 5.9% increase in assault and a 9.1% increase in robbery.

(Sources: National Institute of Justice; Santa Clara County Health Department, 1989; Collins and Messerschmidt, "Epidemiology of Alcohol-Related Violence," Alcohol Health & Research World, 1993; Pacific Center for Violence Prevention, "Policy Brief: Reducing Access to Alcohol," 1995.)

26

CONFRONT WHERE AND HOW ALCOHOL IS SOLD

Policies that control *where* alcohol is sold and *how it is promoted, priced and packaged* are effective at reducing high-risk drinking by youth and adults. "High risk" means excessive drinking or drinking under circumstances that put either the drinker or others in danger of some kind of violence or injury. The most common examples are underage drinking and driving under the influence of alcohol.

1. **Look for the liquor.** What outlets sell alcohol in your community? Note the bars, liquor stores, convenience stores and markets. Evaluate their impact on your community.

2. **Put the pressure on.** If there are too many venues selling alcohol, pressure your city council and community advocacy groups not to allow new outlets.

3. **Be a watchdog.** Organize watchdog groups to make sure stores, bars and restaurants do not sell alcohol to youth, and report those that do. You can also report the use of alcohol and drugs in public places to your police department.

> Parents and neighbors in one Southern California community were successful in pressing for legislation that fines liquor store owners who are caught selling alcohol to minors, and revokes liquor licenses if licensees are charged with three incidents of alcohol sales to minors within a three-year period.

4. **Change zoning laws.** Advocate and pressure for change in your community's zoning and conditional-use permits. For example, make sure that liquor stores and bars are not permitted near schools.

5. **Bust the ads.** Check the billboards and advertising signs in your neighborhood. How many promote beer or other alcohol? Does it seem that the scenery in your neighborhood is dominated by pictures of bottles and cans? Pressure advertising companies and the alcohol industry to change the scenery. Call or write letters to billboard companies asking them to vary the products, and not put so much alcohol advertising in your community.

> **Jesse Ramos, a parent in Boyle Heights, objected to his children seeing 65-foot-tall billboards resembling beer cans on their way to school. He and 60 other parents collected signatures and letters of support from local officials. With the support of the Los Angeles Alliance for a Drug Free Community, they succeeded in having the signs replaced. (LOS ANGELES TIMES, August 6, 1996.)**

27

RID YOUR COMMUNITY OF DRUG ABUSE

After 18 months of doing everything they could to shut down a local crack house, Molly Wetzel and 17 of her Berkeley, California, neighbors, aged three to 65, sued the absentee landlord. A small-claims judge awarded Wetzel and her neighbors $2,000 each. Within two weeks, the owner of the house evicted the drug dealers; within a year, the group got their money. Today the neighborhood is thriving and Wetzel has even formed a group to help neighborhoods across the country fight crime using lawsuits. (Richard Louv, "Renewing Community," *Parents*, January 1996, 40–42.)

Community action is one of the most effective ways of routing drug abuse. Band together with a group of concerned neighbors and consider taking the following steps:

1. **Support prevention and treatment.** Educate children, teenagers and parents about the dangers of drugs and alcohol through neighborhood programs and in schools. Advocate for and support local drug treatment programs for adults and for youth.

2. **Educate people at work.** If you are a business owner or employer, implement policies regarding identification of and intervention with employees who show signs of abusing drugs or alcohol. Educate employees about the dangers of substance abuse in your workplace, and about warning signs and resources for help.

3. **Keep the cops in your corner.** Work with police to organize neighbors to figure out ways to close down drug dealers.

4. **Bring down the house.** Getting rid of crack houses and other points of sale of illegal drugs is a tall order. Yet Wetzel's story shows it can be done. Start by bringing your complaints to the police. Videotape suspected illegal drug activity. Keep a log, including license plate numbers. Observe, then report your observations to the police. Do not try to intervene on your own. If the police do not succeed in routing drug users, you might try to take your complaints to local government. In the case of a crack house, you can sue the landlord.

5. **Get tough on tenants.** If illegal drug sales are going on in your apartment building, pressure the building's owners to take action against the tenants involved in drug activity. Be creative in thinking of ways to get drug dealers to leave. One group of tenants persistently played gospel music until the drug dealers and users became so irritated they left!

6. **If you can't beat 'em—compete with 'em.** Involve large groups of community people in organizing activities to compete with drug dealing in the drug dealers' location. Plan a block party, community fair, neighborhood garage sale or street concert.

> The crack trade moved into the small town of Taylor, Texas, bringing with it violent crime. Residents joined together to form Turn Around Taylor, a community action group whose goal was to take back their town. Members wore jackets with the slogan, "UP WITH HOPE, DOWN WITH DOPE," and demonstrated on streets where the heaviest dealing happened. The organization succeeded in getting the local government to ban public consumption of alcohol in the downtown area and to bulldoze 48 worn-out buildings near the railroad tracks where drug dealers did business. Drug dealers were incarcerated or left town,

and Taylor was turned around. (Richard Lacayo, "Law and Order," TIME, January 15, 1996.)

Resources

Safe Streets Now! is the group Molly Wetzel formed to help neighborhoods fight crime using lawsuits. Based in San Francisco, it has 24 chapters in six states. Call 1-800-404-9100 for information.

National Clearinghouse for Alcohol and Drug Information, 1-800-729-6686.

28

THE THREE Ds: DRINKING, DRUGS AND DRIVING

When Candy Lightner's 13-year-old daughter was killed by a repeat offender drunk driver in 1980, Candy was grief-stricken and enraged. She spoke up, bringing public attention to the fact that about two out of every five Americans will be involved in an alcohol-related car crash at some time in their lives. This was the beginning of Mothers Against Drunk Driving, a national organization that has influenced the passage of more than 2,000 drunk driving laws.

All drugs, including alcohol, alter the mind and interfere with motor skills, hindering judgment, reaction time and perception necessary for safe driving. Anyone can become the victim of a drunk driver, including the driver. Any social or occasional drinker or alcoholic can be the cause of a car accident. Using drugs and alcohol when driving is a deadly combination.

1. **If you drink, don't drive.** If you choose to drink:

   ♦ Eat before you drink and while you are drinking.
   ♦ Set a limit and stick to it.
   ♦ Arrange for someone who will not be drinking to be the "designated driver."

2. **If you serve drinks, do it responsibly.** Set a good example for family members, neighbors and friends:

- Don't force drinks or drugs on guests at a party.
- Pace your serving of drinks.
- Always include nonalcoholic beverages.
- Make the last round nonalcoholic.
- Don't let friends or guests drive when impaired.

3. **Plan for safe driving with teens.** Discuss transportation with teenage drivers before they go out for the evening so that they have alternatives for a safe ride home. Make it absolutely clear that they should never drink or use drugs and drive. Nor should they get in a car with an impaired driver.

4. **Start a safe-rides program.** Safe-rides programs give people who have been drinking a means of alternative transportation. Bartenders, party hosts, organizations and community members publicize the safe-rides phone number. Volunteers answer the phones and transport those who have been drinking or using drugs. Many high schools have safe-rides programs for students.

Resources

Mothers Against Drunk Driving, 1-800-GET-MADD.

Students Against Drunk Driving, (508) 481-3568.

SIGNS OF DRUG OR ALCOHOL ABUSE

Sudden changes in behavior or appearance.

Dramatic changes in sleeping or eating habits.

Frequent moodiness.

Poor performance in school or at work.

Difficulty in concentrating.

Nervousness or agitation.

Loss of energy and/or excessive fatigue.

Secrecy, lying or avoiding friends and family.

Unnecessary risk taking.

Impaired relationships with family or friends.

Drugs, alcohol or items of value missing from home.

Sudden change in choice of friends.

Inexplicably large amounts of money in possession.

29

HELP YOUR CHILD RESIST DRUGS AND ALCOHOL

"Just Say No" is a simplistic solution to a complex problem. Today children as young as seven or eight may be exposed to drugs and alcohol, well before they are even aware of the repercussions. Myrna Shure, Ph.D., author of *Raising a Thinking Child*, says that warning children to just say no "doesn't help children who are frightened of what might happen with their peers if they say no. It also doesn't teach them options to using drugs." So what's a parent or caregiver to do?

1. **Open your ears.** Before you tell children your views on alcohol and drugs, find out what they know and think themselves. Children pick up a lot of information, much of it erroneous. For instance, one woman's seven-year-old didn't know the difference between prescription, nonprescription and illegal drugs. Some questions you might ask:

   ♦ What have you heard about drugs?
   ♦ Who do you get this information from?
   ♦ Is taking drugs a good idea?
   ♦ How do drugs affect people?

   The Parent Resource Institute for Drug Education (PRIDE) in Atlanta, Georgia, organized parents to conduct an in-school survey to learn the truth about the drug problem in their school and community. They then held meetings to inform parents and teachers about the extent of drug use in their community, and to organize workshops and drug awareness weeks.

2. **Discuss—don't lecture.** Have open and honest discussions among family members, where everyone's views are respected. Share information you have researched or know from experience about the effects of alcohol and drugs. Don't assume that because you discuss something once with your children that it is enough.

3. **Lead by example.** Kids need to know what you think about the subject of drugs and alcohol, and that you feel strongly and care about what they do. If you use alcohol, make sure you act as responsibly as you would like your children to. Be prepared to answer tough questions like "Did you ever do drugs?" or "Why can't we drink if you drink?"

4. **Help take the pressure off.** You may find that your children's friends have a positive influence on them, or a destructive influence. With good self-esteem and good refusal skills, children can resist negative peer pressure. The pressures around them can make it difficult even for the strongest kids. Help your children make good decisions for themselves. For example, prepare them to deal with not being like the other kids, and applaud their courage not to conform. Practice with them the steps they can take to say no to their peers. Refusal skills to practice are:

   ♦ State your feelings using "I" statements: "I don't feel like having a beer."
   ♦ Give a consequence: "If I do, I'll get grounded."
   ♦ Offer an alternative: "I'm going to just stick with this soda."
   ♦ Leave the scene: "I think I'm going to head home now."
   ♦ Don't antagonize anyone: "So I'll see you tomorrow, OK?"
   ♦ Talk it over with someone you trust afterwards if you need help sorting out your feelings.

5. **Set firm rules and limits.** For example, be consistent about family rules about drinking. In most cities it is illegal for teens to drink alcohol, so allowing drinking at home but not in public is inconsistent, giving a mixed message. A clear rule

for teens about drinking is "no drinking allowed." Discuss how to handle the rules.

6. **Get strength in numbers.** Talk with your children's friends and their parents about setting up curfews and guidelines for having alcohol- and drug-free parties and school events.

7. **Make "Drug-Free" enticing.** Encourage your children's involvement in activities, sports, hobbies, civic involvement and other interests which lessen tendencies towards substance abuse. Better yet, make drug-free parties seem the hip thing to do.

> **Fighting Back is Santa Barbara's unique community-run program to fight alcohol and drug abuse. One of their most popular activities has turned out to be the social event of the year, attracting 8,000 youths. Held annually, it's called "I'm free for the weekend," and it begins with students pledging to stay alcohol- and drug-free for three days. A small purple wristband entitles a student to a host of free and discounted services and entertainment. In 1996, 150 Santa Barbara businesses chipped in, and bus rides to and from the event were free. (David Holstrom, "Santa Barbara Aims to Knock Drug Abuse by 'Fighting Back,'" CHRISTIAN SCIENCE MONITOR, December 2, 1996)**

Resources

Parent Resource Institute for Drug Education (PRIDE), (770) 458-9900, http://www.prideusa.org.

"A Parent's Guide to Prevention" is a helpful pamphlet from Partnership for a Drug Free America, 1-800-624-0100.

"Working it Out: A Survival Guide for Kids," is an instructional video that is part of the Personal Safety Series, produced by PSI Productions, 22 Brigham Hill Road, Essex Junction, VT 05451, (802) 879-1850.

WHAT TO DO WHEN YOUR CHILD DRINKS OR TAKES DRUGS

Don't overreact or panic if your child experiments with alcohol or drugs. How you deal with it may influence his or her attitude and how he or she deals with it.

If you find that your child has been using drugs or alcohol on a regular basis, confront him or her with detailed accounts of times and occasions when he or she used drugs and alcohol, his or her irregular behavior and effects on the family. Make a commitment and insist that you all seek help together.

Organize a meeting with concerned family and friends, teachers, counselors and other professionals to create a uniform plan of action.

Seek support from local substance abuse programs to gather necessary information.

Resources
Center for Substance Abuse Treatment, 1-800-662-HELP.

National Helpline (for drug problems), 1-800-HELP-111.

Alcoholics Anonymous World Services, (212) 890-3400.

Alanon/Alateen Family Group Headquarters, Inc., 1-800-356-9996.

YOUTH VIOLENCE

DO YOU KNOW . . .

. . . THE FACTS ABOUT YOUTH AND GUNS?

◆ Every day in the United States 16 children are killed in gun-related homicides, suicides and accidents.

◆ One in 25 high school students carried a gun in 1990.

◆ Every six hours, a youth between 10 and 19 years old commits suicide with a gun.

◆ For 15- to 24-year-olds, one of four deaths was caused by firearms.

◆ Among African-American youths aged 15 to 19 years old, 60% of deaths for males and 22% of deaths for females were from firearms, compared to 23% and 10% among white males and females.

◆ Juvenile homicides involving firearms nearly tripled from 1984 to 1994.

(Sources: California Wellness Foundation, 1996; Pacific Center for Violence Prevention, "Preventing Youth Violence," 1994; Center to Prevent Handgun Violence.)

30

KEEP KIDS AWAY FROM GUNS

The prevalence of and easy access to guns has become a critical issue for our youth. While kids say they want guns, often for protection, it is an illusion that guns keep them safe. Schools can install state-of-the-art metal detectors. They can put a squad of security guards on patrol or institute stiff penalties for carrying guns. Yet, these deterrents must work hand-in-hand with a more fundamental action: confronting kids' belief that guns will keep them safe.

1. **Show them alternatives.** Talk to children about ways to solve arguments and fights without guns or violence. Push for antigun school curricula in the schools and for student-run conflict resolution programs in which students help mediate other students' disputes.

   > Farideh Kioumehr of Los Angeles was disturbed when her 10-year-old son returned from a party with a realistic-looking plastic rifle. "Guns are for killing, toys are for playing," she said. "The two shouldn't be mixed together." She organized the Anti-Violence Day Project to speak with children and their parents, asking the children to give up their toy guns and use them to create a piece of art or a billboard advertising the dangers of guns. In return, the organization awards the children a certificate and a T-shirt. (LOS ANGELES TIMES, May 8, 1996.)
   >
   > The program "This Is My Neighborhood—No Shooting Allowed" was created in South Bend, Indiana, in 1993 to teach children alternative ways to solve problems and gain protection from violence. The project devel-

oped into a community-wide volunteer effort to enable children to change the attitudes of their peers about gun violence and build pride in their neighborhoods. It has reached 7,000 school-age children in classrooms. ("A Community's Answer to Teen Violence," CHILDREN TODAY, 1994, 20–24.)

2. **Make your presence known.** When kids don't feel safe en route to school, in school halls or even on the block, adults must establish a visible presence. Not just moms, but dads too, are getting involved in protecting neighborhood youth. The idea to stress is that *people* can keep you safe—not guns.

   At Glen Oaks High School in Baton Rouge, Lousiana, the Security Dads, a group of about 50 concerned dads, take shifts patrolling the halls and provide a listening ear or comfortable shoulder for kids with problems. A similar group in Omaha, Nebraska, Mad Dads, patrols drug-ridden streets with walkie-talkies and cellular phones. The group has expanded to 45 chapters in 13 states. (Marilyn Gardner, "Neighborhood Defense: Watchful Eyes, Caring Hearts," CHRISTIAN SCIENCE MONITOR, October 21, 1996, 10–12; Jeanne DeQuine, "Mad Dads Patrol the Streets to Drive Out Drug Dealers, Violence," CHRISTIAN SCIENCE MONITOR, September 19, 1996, 13.)

3. **Establish safe homes.** For instance, the National McGruff House Safety Program establishes neighborhood homes as reliable sources of help if youth are threatened or lost. The participating homes display a sign featuring McGruff, the Crime Dog.

4. **Let reality be a teacher.** In a *USA Today* survey during a National Association of Student Councils conference, teens said that the best way to drive lessons home is to use real-life stories. Arrange for someone who has suffered as the result of gun violence to give a talk in your community.

Lorna Hawkins started Drive By Agony after she lost two sons to gun violence. The group provides support to families of victims of gun violence. They sponsor marches and speak-outs, and talk with youths about real tragedies that come from gun violence.

Resources

The Straight Talk About Risks (STAR) Program was started by the Center to Prevent Handgun Violence to teach youth alternatives to using guns. For information about their program curriculum for use in your family or community, contact them at 1225 Eye Street, N.W., Suite 1100, Washington, DC 20005, (202) 289-7319.

McGruff House Safety Programs of the National Crime Prevention Council, 1700 K Street, N.W., 2nd floor, Washington, DC 20006-3817, (202) 466-6272.

Drive By Agony, P.O. Box 762, Lynwood, CA 91262, (310) 537-8018.

31

. . . AND KEEP GUNS AWAY FROM KIDS

1. **Start at home.** Of course, the safest thing is not to have a gun in your home, especially not a handgun. If you choose to keep a gun, empty it, lock it up and keep it well out of reach of children. You might even consider using a trigger-locking device. Lock and store bullets in a separate location. But locking up a gun is not enough. You need to:

   ♦ Teach everyone gun safety guidelines appropriate to their age and ability. For instance, very young children only need to know that guns are dangerous and should never be touched.
   ♦ Tell children to stay clear of guns when they are in the homes of friends. Instruct them to leave the premises immediately and to return home.
   ♦ Explain that gun violence on television and in the movies is not real. In real life, people are hurt and killed with guns. Give real-life examples.

2. **Organize antigun events.** Community campaigns that educate teens and efforts to reduce gun availability have been extraordinarily successful. Here are a few ideas:

   ♦ Start a "turn-in" or "buy-back" campaign, such as the one started by Eleanor Montana of Mothers and Men Against Violence in Wilmington, California: "Give your mother a Mother's Day present—turn in your gun on Mother's Day!" Youth were given gift certificates to local merchants—"Buy Back Certificates"—in exchange for their guns.
   ♦ Campaign to get the police department to destroy guns they have confiscated instead of selling them at an auction.

- Display a "You are welcome—Your gun is not" sticker in the window of your home or business.
- Hold a memorial event in memory of a victim of gun violence as a community-organizing campaign.
- Pressure local school administration and students to make school a gun-free zone. Schools that are gun-free zones have clear and sensible consequences for students who bring a gun or other weapon to school.
- Focus public attention on manufacturers of guns in your community in order to pressure them to stop manufacturing weapons, such as handguns, that are designed to kill people. For example, in Los Angeles, a coalition of community groups and parents who have lost children organized a Ring of Fire protest march from one gun manufacturer to another.

> **After three shootings shattered his family, South Boston's Michael McDonald dedicated himself to helping communities get rid of handguns. His Citizens for Safety's most effective public effort so far is a gun buy-back program that removed 2,600 handguns from Boston streets in the last three years. When McDonald publicized that his group was offering $50 for a gun, no questions asked, money from private organizations began pouring in. Citizens for Safety collected over $65,000 to support their gun buy-back and other violence prevention campaigns. (David Holmstrom, "One Family's Trials Spur a Commitment to Community Safety," CHRISTIAN SCIENCE MONITOR, October 7, 1996, 10–12.)**

3. **Support legislation to prevent gun violence.** Pressure local, state and federal government to:

- Promote mandatory gun and ammunition registration systems.
- Impose strict security and zoning requirements on gun dealers in your community.

- Prohibit the sale of "junk guns" which are low-quality, easily concealed handguns. Junk guns are favored for use in crimes, and are too poorly made to be valuable for any legitimate use.
- Tax gun and ammunition sales to help allay the large public costs of gun violence.

Resources

Women Against Gun Violence, (310) 204-2348, operates a campaign to educate, organize and mobilize women to end gun violence. They sponsor a speaker's bureau and actions to focus public attention on the problem, and they educate legislators and the media.

Pacific Center for Violence Prevention, San Francisco General Hospital, San Francisco, CA 94110, (415) 285-1793.

WHAT IS A STREET GANG?

Street gangs are groups of youths who join together to achieve a sense of belonging, for ethnic affiliation, for protection from other neighborhood youths and to engage in violent and criminal activities. Children as young as nine years old are involved in gangs. Older members in their thirties and forties who are no longer actively participating in violence may still have influence and authority within gangs. Most gang members are teens.

Not all groups of teenagers hanging out together or forming groups that have a strong sense of belonging are drug-dealing, violent street gangs. Street gangs, however, form bonds around committing violent crimes and expect members to participate in violence.

32

MOBILIZE AGAINST GANG VIOLENCE

A young man drove his Jeep Cherokee into an Omaha, Nebraska, gas station. Because the color of his car matched a rival gang's colors, the man was jumped and badly beaten by gang members. Gang violence is senseless to those of us watching from the outside, but to youth in gangs violence is a way of life and a bond. When we mobilize to fight against gang violence, we must not only counter the violence itself but address the sense of belonging, the sense of purpose and identity, and the self-esteem that being in a street gang offers to its young members. But we cannot overlook or simplify the complex factors that keep gangs flourishing, such as easy access to drugs, limited economic opportunities and the debilitating effects of poverty.

1. **Read—and erase—the writing on the wall.** In order to fight gang violence, you must first identify it. One of the first signs of the presence of a gang in a neighborhood is graffiti. When translated, graffiti can give community members a great deal of information. *Read, record* and *remove* are the three *R*s at San Diego Unified School District. Schools in this district photograph any graffiti on campus since graffiti can be used to resolve school crimes or track criminal trends on campus. Other signs of gang presence in your community are:

   ♦ Hand signals, signs and clothes for different gangs.
   ♦ Hangouts for local gangs, such as fast-food drive-throughs, liquor stores, abandoned buildings, crack houses and certain public telephones used for drug commerce.

- Incidents of crime that may be gang-related, such as shakedowns of younger children for money, drug dealing and robberies.

2. **Grapple with gangs.** Organize alliances or task forces to collaborate with experienced gang prevention organizations and juvenile police teams.

   Maria Teixeira of the Committee for Peace/Comite por Paz (a project of Proyecto Pastoral) brings together parents in East Los Angeles public housing projects to organize activities and solve problems. They promote unity in the face of gang intimidation. They build alliances with former gang members and current leaders who have influence within gangs to reduce the violence.

3. **Keep the peace.** Encourage truces between gangs that are hostile to one another. Involve gang leaders or former gang members in negotiations to promote nonviolence commitments by gang members. They can be motivated because they also suffer from violence and loss of lives among their members, relatives and friends.

   The mothers of Pico-Aliso in East Los Angeles, California, form a picket line they call "love marches," every Friday night on a corner where youth and children have died from gang violence. "We approach it with love: 'It's because we love you that we want you to stop shooting.' If gang members know us, and we know the gang members, it's hard to shoot." Natividad Lopez urges mothers to defy and embrace the gang members who shoot at one another. (LOS ANGELES TIMES, October 8, 1995.)

4. **Create opportunities for belonging.** Generate activities to engage young people that provide a high sense of involvement and accomplishment.

Venice for a Positive Change is a Southern California group that provides career mentoring, tutoring and job placement. They also sponsor softball games at the local park and training programs at a youth skills center. Two years before the group was formed, gun battles raged between two gangs in Venice and long-time residents were afraid to walk down the street or take their kids to the park. A gang truce and the efforts of groups such as Venice for a Positive Change are credited with ending the reign of terror. (LOS ANGELES TIMES, June 10, 1996.)

THE WARNING SIGNS OF GANG INVOLVEMENT

Graffiti writing or lettering on personal property that seems obsessive and pervasive. Graffiti marks out turf, serves as a challenge to rival gangs and also communicates messages between gangs.

Clothing—gangs may favor certain colors or types of clothing, such as bandanas, hats or team jackets.

Talking in slang.

Tattoos—particular tattoos that have names of the gang or symbols that show loyalty and pride in the gang.

Jewelry—some gangs wear identifying jewelry, such as chains, earrings or finger rings.

Friends who are known gang members—if you don't know, check it out.

Tag nickname in graffiti on public property.

Hand signals and signs.

Signs of drug or alcohol abuse.

Suddenly having a lot of money from unexplainable sources.

Truancies from school.

Changes in grades.

33

KEEP KIDS OUT OF GANGS

Active families are key to keeping kids out of gangs. Every effort that strengthens your child's bonds to your family, school and positive influences in your community helps to innoculate against gang involvement.

1. **Look under your own roof.** Children who are attracted to gangs, "wannabes," can be reached and diverted before they become immersed in hard-core gang culture. Know the warning signs of gang involvement. Some aspects of youth culture, such as music and dress, mimic and glamorize gang culture. Be alert to changes in your child's behavior and friends, and recognize the difference between participating in popular youth culture and actual involvement in a violent gang.

    If your child is already in a gang, don't give up. It is possible to leave a gang. Find out everything you can from police, schools, coaches, social workers and your child's friends. Confront your child's gang-related behavior, for example, dress, hostile attitude and truancy. Pay attention to what your child needs that will strengthen his or her ability to resist the gang.

    You may need to change your child's school, move, involve people who have a positive influence on him or her, and seek support from agencies, such as antigang community organizations, probation and law enforcement.

2. **Deglamorize gangs.**

    ◆ As a family, discuss the dangers of gang involvement.
    ◆ Show your children examples of consequences of gang

involvement. Tell stories about victims of gang violence. Introduce children to reformed gang members.

- ♦ Provide positive ways for your children to spend their time.
- ♦ Introduce them to other groups, such as athletic teams and youth empowerment groups.

3. **Teach by example.** If there are gang members in your family, recognize their influence on your children. If they want to help you keep your children out of gangs, have them talk to your children about the realities of fear and violence they experienced. If they glamorize gang involvement, make every effort possible to keep them away from your children.

4. **Be involved.** Stay involved in your children's lives. Know what is going on at school and after school. Meet their friends. Help them enroll in job training or mentor programs that give them healthy alternatives for strengthening their self-esteem.

> Because of KYDS (Keep Youth Doing Something), San Fernando Valley families can give their children alternatives to joining the local drug-dealing gangs. KYDS is a coed youth recreational and educational program that sponsors a softball league that plays an All-Star game against the local Los Angeles Police Department team. They have career days, community clean-up days and tours of local colleges. Local businesses are actively involved. Youth interact informally with adults who are positive role models.

FACTS ON TEEN DATING VIOLENCE

Researchers estimate that 28% of students have experienced physical violence in a romantic relationship.

Studies on date rape indicate that 67% of young women reporting rape were assaulted in a dating situation.

Teen relationship violence happens everywhere—in large cities and rural towns.

It occurs in every culture and ethnic group.

It happens in gay and lesbian as well as heterosexual relationships. It happens to teens who have babies and to those who do not. It happens to teens who live together and to those who live with their parents.

The potential for murder is present in every violent relationship. According to the FBI, 20% of homicide victims are between the ages of 15 and 24, and one out of every three women murdered in the United States is killed by a husband or a boyfriend.

Although young men are also victims and young women are also violent, the social tolerance for boys to be aggressive towards girls makes it far more common for boys to be violent.

34

CONFRONT TEEN RELATIONSHIP VIOLENCE

A sharp "shut up" and threat of physical harm, a slap on the face, forced sexual activity—dating violence affects up to 28% of teenagers in an intimate relationship. Yet, perhaps more alarming is the silence that accompanies dating violence. In a recent study conducted by the University of Illinois at a Chicago high school, only 4% of the students who experienced some form of dating violence told an authority figure.

Many of the victims of teen relationship violence believe that their partners' violence is a sign of love. Girls feel pressure to have a boyfriend in order to be popular, and many girls feel that having an abusive boyfriend is better than being alone. Teen relationship violence must be prevented in order to protect our children, and to keep battered girlfriends from growing up to be battered wives and battering boyfriends from continuing their violence into adulthood.

1. **Observe.** Because teens don't talk to adults about their relationship problems, adults must observe, ask questions, be available and respond quickly to signs of violence. Even if a girl denies any violence, make sure she knows what to do in an emergency, and that you will pick her up anywhere, any-time, no questions asked.

2. **Intervene.** If you see a violent incident, or a pattern of abuse, *do something*. Bring it to public attention. When we ignore a

violent incident, we unintentionally convey a powerful message to the victim and the perpetrator that it's no big deal.

> Sara's boyfriend, Richard, followed her to the mall, and became enraged when she met a friend. He stormed over, grabbed her hair and slammed her against a wall. A salesperson ran over, yelled, "Stop! Leave her alone!" and called to her coworker to call mall security and 911. Richard was stunned, let go of Sara, turned and ran. Later Sara reported that she was grateful and surprised that anyone took Richard's violence seriously.

3. **Educate.** Work with your local schools and others to develop dating violence prevention curricula, response systems and policies to address this problem.

   ♦ Push for prevention curricula aimed at grades six through 12. The best programs break down stereotypes and myths and teach that relationship violence is not normal. They teach boys to be respectful, and teach girls not to tolerate verbal or physical abuse or coerced sex. They promote healthy relationship skills and nonviolent conflict resolution.
   ♦ Set standards for nonviolent behavior, with clear consequences for their violation in schools. For example, bench abusive athletes in your high school.
   ♦ Facilitate coordination among youth-serving agencies, including the juvenile police, to ensure a response to relationship violence.

4. **Reach out to boyfriends.** Develop new or promote existing programs that are accessible to teens who are violent, who have shown early signs of becoming violent or who have been victimized. Start teen violence prevention support groups in schools, clubs or youth groups.

5. **Raise awareness.** Inform the community that domestic violence starts early and that stopping it requires prevention and intervention with youth. Make sure that hotline numbers and information about the warning signs of abuse are available wherever young people and parents congregate.

> **To begin talking about the problem, the town of Lincoln, Nebraska, tried a novel approach. Teenagers, counselors, parents, legislators and police discussed dating violence in a televised town meeting. The response was overwhelming. Local crisis centers received an enormous number of calls from parents, churches, schools and young women, all saying, "Tell us more, what can we do?" (Lynn Harris, "The Hidden World of Dating Violence," PARADE, September 22, 1996, 4–6.)**

Resources

The Los Angeles Commission on Assaults Against Women has logged more than 2,800 requests for its classroom curriculum on dating violence, In Touch with Teens. *Write to them at 6043 Hollywood Boulevard, Suite 200, Los Angeles, CA 90028, (213) 462-1281.*

In Love and In Danger *and* What Parents Need to Know About Dating Violence, *written by the authors, are available from Seal Press (see the back of this book for more information).*

35

GIVE YOUTH A CHANCE

Given a choice, would kids want to hang out at the mall, drink alcohol and commit vandalism or learn how to take care of an armadillo? Moorhead, Minnesota, a college town of 32,000, found out the surprising answer was the latter. Moorhead Healthy Community Initiative (MHCI) is one of a few pioneering programs trying to supplant a popular but dysfunctional idea: Find out what's wrong with youth and stamp it out. Instead, MCHI aims to build on youth assets rather than shortcomings and takes its cue from youth, not adults. For instance, before designing after-school activities, the project surveyed 1,100 fourth through eighth graders to find out what they preferred to do. The number one choice: working with animals. (David Holmstrom, "Asset-Building: A City Mobilizes Around Kids," *Christian Science Monitor*, November 4, 1996, 10–12.)

The lesson: *Youth deserve respect just like we do.* Give them a chance and:

1. **Stop stereotyping.** Recognize kids' diversity and individuality. Look beyond their clothing, hair and music, and relate to them as individuals. Youth who dress so that they look menacing, for example, by wearing black leather or gang clothing, may not really be as hard as they look.

   When 20 gang members showed up uninvited at Norma Montgomery's neighborhood block party, the Southern California mother of three did a surprising thing. She invited them to the party. She told them they were welcome to join but that none of their gang activities would be tolerated. Ms. Montgomery asked them their names, and they replied. They sat down and ate, and said thank you when they left. The following year they returned, bringing more friends with them. "They were just so nice," Montgomery recalls. (Marilyn Gardner, "Neighborhood Defense: Watchful Eyes, Caring Hearts," CHRISTIAN SCIENCE MONITOR, October 21, 1996, 10–12.)

2. **Hire a helping hand.** Hire local youth to work or intern in your business or organization. Organize local businesses to hire youths for after-school and summer jobs. Find ways to provide on-the-job training for youth who have no job experience.

3. **Play ball.** Start or support an athletics program or a sports team for youth in the neighborhood.

> Charles Garcia of New York City was frustrated because his daughter, who loved baseball, could not find a place to play ball in their neighborhood. He started a girls' softball team at a nearby park, which grew to become a league with teams throughout their city.

4. **Turn spare time into care time.** In the unstructured hours between the "school's out" bell and 6:00 p.m., young people often lack adult supervision—and idleness can lead to trouble. Start or support after-school or weekend classes, tutoring or other activities for children and youth.

> As drugs and violence have become more prevalent in inner cities, many black churches have stepped forward to offer children a safe haven. About 45 churches in 12 American cities offer a program sponsored by the Congress of National Black Churches. Project SPIRIT is an after-school tutorial and life-skills

program designed to build self-esteem, provide cultural appreciation and bolster a child's capacity to do well in life and school. SPIRIT is an acronym for Strength, Perseverance, Imagination, Responsibility, Integrity and Talent. (David Holmstrom, "Black Churches Put 'Spirit' into Children's Afternoons," CHRISTIAN SCIENCE MONITOR, November 4, 1996, 11–12.)

Cynthia Brown of Cleveland, Ohio, was distressed when her son's friends distracted him from doing his homework in the afternoons. So she invited them to come over and study together. They brought their homework, and she brought the pizza. Within a year, she had expanded to the nearby recreation center to accommodate the number of students and moms who showed up to help.

36

THE MAGIC OF MENTORS

When Washington, D.C., youth Sean Varner met John Hogan through Mentors Inc., he lived in a homeless shelter, was failing at McKinley High School and thinking of dropping out. With Hogan's encouragement and support, Varner gradually turned his life around. His grades improved, his attendance went up and he began to have aspirations for college and a career in engineering.

Youth observe and look to adults for ways to be effective in their personal, social and work lives. Having caring adults in their lives allows young people to think about their options, choices and decisions. Having adults in addition to parents in their lives gives them a variety of perspectives and multiple sources of encouragement.

1. **Be a mentor.** Being a role model or mentor does not require a perfect person or celebrity. Mentors listen to their partners and offer their own realities, their weaknesses and their strengths. Most importantly, they are available to youth who may not have adults around who are consistently willing to listen to or guide them. Find out about mentoring programs in your area, such as Big Brothers and Big Sisters or Boy and Girl Scouts. Volunteer in existing programs, or start one if there isn't one.

   Las Madrinas, a professional women's group with 21 members, has been providing role models for seventh through twelfth graders for 10 years. One student, Dana Garcia, age 16, said she was inspired by Las

Madrinas to become a lawyer. (LOS ANGELES TIMES, January 18, 1996.)

2. **Follow time-tested mentoring DOs and DON'Ts.** Mentors can make a real difference in the lives of their young partners. Yet, a bad mentoring relationship or experience can be more harmful than none at all. Here are some guidelines:

   ◆ Do listen first and then talk.
   ◆ Don't make promises you can't keep.
   ◆ Don't try to follow a preconceived agenda; instead follow your young partner's lead.
   ◆ Don't be too impatient to make a difference; focus on building a relationship first.
   ◆ Do be willing to work harder than your partner at forging a bond.
   ◆ Don't be discouraged if your partner is more lax than you about connecting.
   ◆ Don't ask personal questions before you have a solid relationship.
   ◆ Do be dependable.
   ◆ Don't focus on establishing a relationship with the youth's family members.
   ◆ Do provide support and challenge; don't tell your partner what to do—help him or her work out a problem.
   ◆ Do be sensitive to cultural and economic differences.
   ◆ Do be realistic; you may not turn someone's life around, but you can make a small, worthwhile difference.

3. **Encourage your own children to have mentors.** Whatever their backgrounds, all youth need mentors and models. Make sure your own children have adult role models and mentors with whom they can establish a relationship. And let your children develop this relationship without interference from you or your partner.

   Michael Gibson, 20 years old, said, "At 16, my future was either death or jail." But mentor Martin Jacks

turned his life around. "He basically provided me with a role model, confidant, teacher and somebody, well, just a friend." Today, Gibson is finishing his first year of community college with a 3.75 grade point average, and this fall, he plans to be an English major at a four-year university. (LOS ANGELES TIMES, March 6, 1996.)

Resources

National One to One Partnership, Inc. provides information about mentoring, (202) 338-3844.

Marc Freedman, The Kindness of Strangers: Adult Mentors, Urban Youth, and the New Volunteerism, *San Francisco: Jossey-Bass Publishers, 1993.*

In California, there is a statewide hotline for volunteers to obtain referrals for nearby mentor programs: 1-800-444-3066.

VIOLENCE AGAINST WOMEN

DO YOU KNOW . . .

. . . THE REALITIES ABOUT VIOLENCE AGAINST WOMEN?

Mistaken information and beliefs about sexual and domestic violence persist and are detrimental to productive thinking about these issues. You should know the following:

◆ The American Medical Association calls sexual assault "America's silent epidemic."

◆ More than 70% of rapes of women and girls are committed by persons known to the victim.

◆ Although women may dress to attract male attention, they never ask to be raped by the way they dress.

◆ Violence against wives and girlfriends is serious, and thousands of women in the U.S. are murdered by their "loved one."

◆ The risk for serious injury or murder increases when battered women try to separate or have recently left the batterer.

◆ Domestic violence includes physical assault as well as emotional and verbal abuse, such as constant humiliation or name-calling.

◆ In surveys, young men have reported that rape is acceptable under some circumstances. A majority report that they would force sex if they knew they would not be caught, and a substantial minority admit to having committed sexual violence.

◆ Rape is the most underreported crime.

37

ASSESS THE SAFETY OF YOUR RELATIONSHIP

As tapes of Nicole Brown Simpson calling 911 for help were played over and over on national radio and television, domestic violence hotlines all over the country were inundated with calls from people identifying with the terror they heard. For many, it was the first time they reached out for help.

Many victims don't recognize they are being abused in an intimate relationship. You or someone you know may believe that the abuse is normal, that all relationships contain some abuse or that a lover's hitting or jealous explosions are a measure of love. Or it may seem that the abuser is not really abusive, but "going through a hard time" and, with enough love, will change. These beliefs are part of the cycle of violence in abusive relationships. Assess your relationship. Have you been denying or minimizing a serious problem?

1. **You know you're in trouble when . . .** If any one of the following is true about your relationship, and especially if more than three are true, you need to get help now. Help might be in the form of counseling or in the form of making a plan to safeguard your life. Are you:

   ✓ Afraid of your partner's explosive temper?
   ✓ Being hit, kicked, choked or shoved? Have you had objects thrown at you?
   ✓ Being subjected to verbal abuse, name-calling or constant criticism?

✓ Being threatened with violence towards yourself or someone else, or suicide?

✓ Being watched, followed, checked-up on, stalked or called
constantly?

✓ Becoming isolated from friends and family?

✓ Restricted by your partner's excessive jealousy and posses-
siveness?

✓ Afraid of saying no to sex?

2. **Plan for your safety** if you are in an abusive relationship.

   ♦ **Contact** a domestic violence program and stay in touch as
   you plan for safety.

   ♦ **Pack a bag** with money, keys, copies of important papers,
   a change of clothes and anything you or your children
   would need in an emergency. Place it in a safe, hidden
   place that you can access quickly if you need to leave in a
   hurry.

   ♦ **Keep on hand phone numbers** of emergency resources,
   such as family members, friends and a 24-hour hotline.

   ♦ **Pinpoint dangerous situations** and locations in which you
   might be especially vulnerable to relationship violence, for
   example, driving home after a party. Think through various
   safety action plans for such situations.

3. **It's not over when it's over.** Leaving an abusive relationship is
really only the first step on the way to healing. Victims of
abuse may still fear for their lives, and yet, they may succumb
to extreme pressure to go back. You need to take extreme
measures to avoid contact.

   ♦ **Resist the pressure** to go back:

   > Keep and look at photos of your injuries.

   > Use 24-hour domestic violence hotlines.

   > Get counseling.

   > Build your support systems.

- ♦ **Avoid telephone contact:**
  - Change your phone number.
  - Screen calls with an answering machine.
  - Use a pager or cellular phone.
  - Save tapes of harassing or threatening calls.
  - Unplug phones at night after everyone gets home.
- ♦ **Change locks and install alarms.**
- ♦ **Alert people to your comings and goings.**
- ♦ **Get a restraining order** (order of protection).
- ♦ **Join a support group.**
- ♦ **Relocate or seek refuge** in a battered women's shelter. Shelters provide safety and confidentiality, counseling, support, referrals, and can help with all aspects of the process of becoming empowered and safe.

Lorie and Jason were dating for three months when Lorie realized that Jason flew into a jealous rage every time she went out with her friends. She talked to Jason about the kind of trust she wanted in a relationship. After a couple of weeks, she realized that he was seriously limiting her life outside of their relationship. She talked to a friend who had a healthy-relationship checklist, and saw the potential for abuse. She broke up with Jason and told him to get some help.

Resources

National Domestic Violence Hotline, 1-800-799-SAFE; TDD, 1-800-787-3224.

National Resource Center on Domestic Violence, 1-800-537-2238.

Family Violence Prevention Fund, 383 Rhode Island Street, Suite 304, San Francisco, CA 94103, (415) 252-8900, fax (415) 252-8991, http://www.fvpf.org/fund, email: fund@igc.apc.org.

38

TAKE PERSONAL RESPONSIBILITY FOR STOPPING RAPE

Only rapists actually commit rape—true. But we all share a responsibility for building a culture in which rape is never tolerated. Do you—or others you know—accept images of women as victims, or sometimes say that a woman who is assaulted "should have known better"? If so, it's time to start thinking differently. Changing your own attitudes, and influencing others in your life to change theirs, makes a difference in changing our society's tolerance for rape.

1. **What everyone can do:**

   ♦ Boycott products, magazines, movies or music that glamorize rape or woman-bashing—better yet, let companies whose products you boycott know the reasons behind your decision not to purchase.
   ♦ Don't perpetuate stereotypes about male and female sex roles.
   ♦ Contact your local rape crisis center and rape prevention program. Offer your support or donation. Become a volunteer.
   ♦ Advocate for strong antirape programs and rape crisis centers through your local, state and federal legislators.
   ♦ Educate yourself on the myths and realities of rape.
   ♦ Don't blame women for the violence perpetrated against them.
   ♦ Take responsibility for your own sexuality. Don't let it be

defined by your partner, the media, peer pressure or anyone else.

+ Communicate with your partner about sex.

2. What men can do:

+ Don't tell or laugh at woman-bashing or rape jokes.
+ Don't get a woman drunk or give her drugs in order to have sex with her.
+ Base sexual relations on a firm yes. Seek consent.
+ Tell other men that silence does not equal consent.
+ If you see or hear other men treating a woman badly, speak up. Become an ally for that woman.
+ Educate male youths around you that forcing a woman or girl to have sex through coercion or threats is rape, and is unacceptable.
+ Respect the experiences of rape survivors, and join them in participating in community efforts to stop rapists and to educate others.

3. What women can do:

+ Develop skills to resist pressure to have sex against your will. Communicate no clearly.
+ Don't drink or do drugs beyond your ability to control your body or your environment.
+ Take a women's self-defense class.
+ Be aware that rape can happen to any woman at any time.
+ Be aware of your environment so that you can minimize your risk.
+ If you have been a victim of sexual assault by a stranger, acquaintance or intimate, know that there is help out there. Seek it.

Resources
Rape, Abuse and Incest National Network (RAINN), 1-800-656-4673, connects you directly to a local rape crisis center hotline.

39

STOP SEXUAL HARASSMENT ON THE JOB

Taking action to confront sexual harassment is the best way to stop it. If you are subjected to advances or sexual suggestions that affect the security of your job, or if you see that a coworker is being harassed, bring it out into the open.

1. **Know sexual harassment when you see it.** Sexual harassment includes unwelcome sexual advances, requests for sexual favors and other verbal or physical conduct of a sexual nature. *Behavior is considered sexual harassment when:*

   ♦ Submission is a term or condition of employment.
   ♦ Submission to or rejection of sexual advances is used as the basis for employment decisions (affecting the person being harassed).
   ♦ The behavior has the effect of unreasonably interfering with a person's work performance.
   ♦ The behavior creates an intimidating, hostile or offensive working environment.

2. **Prepare yourself.** Take steps to ensure your own safety as you prepare to take action against sexual harassment. Sometimes reporting harassment leads to retaliation or other stressful changes in treatment by others at work. Sometimes the report is not believed; sometimes nothing is done.

   ♦ Ask for help from people in your support system—at work and outside of work.
   ♦ Take precautions regarding your safety. For example, take precautions not to be alone with the harasser.

- Find out what protections are provided by company policies and personnel.
- Document any changes, comments or actions by the harasser or others that might be related to your reporting harassment.
- Explore your options: What will you do if your environment at work becomes intolerable? Knowing your options can give you more strength.

3. **Take matters in your own hands** and:

- Verbally confront the harasser.
- Write a letter to the harasser, containing a factual account of each incident, a description of how harassment has affected you and a clear statement that you want the incidents to STOP.
- Keep a journal.
- Tell other people about the harassment.

4. **Make a formal complaint** to your employer or take legal action, for example:

- File a report with your state Fair Employment and Housing Department or appropriate authority.
- File a report with the federal Equal Employment Opportunity Commission.
- File a sexual harassment lawsuit against the employer.

NOTE: All of the above suggestions also apply to students in an educational setting.

40

TAKE ACTION WITH YOUR COMMUNITY

In numbers there is strength. People joining together can make it more difficult for violence against women to continue. Every person, no matter what their position or professional status, can take steps to expand the community safety net for victims and to take a stand against violence.

1. **Don't ignore violence.** Become an ally for a victim. If you see or hear any evidence of sexual assault or domestic violence, write down information, call the police, alert others in the vicinity and intervene in whatever way you can without putting yourself in danger.

2. **Accept no excuses.** Judges, prosecutors and counselors as well as battered women must stop accepting apologies or excuses from violent men. As a community member, you can:

   ♦ Join others to pressure the criminal justice system, professionals and fellow community members to take all violence seriously. Consequences must be known by everyone: Assaults should result in arrest and prosecution.
   ♦ Mobilize others to influence better coordination, for example, by joining a community police advisory committee or a volunteer court watch program.

   In 1979, D. Diane Miller's husband played Russian roulette with a gun held to her head. The police didn't do anything to protect her, and her frustrating experiences with the courts led her to decide to do something to change the system. She started going to court

to observe how judges decided cases involving battered women. She sold her jewelry to keep going, and her watchdog efforts grew into the volunteer Courtwatch program in Los Angeles, which now has 90 volunteers who monitor the criminal and family courts and volunteer attorneys who help battered women get justice.

3. **Educate yourself and others.** Invite speakers and have meetings to learn about sexual and domestic violence in your apartment building, condominium or neighborhood.

   Vecinos Unidos/Neighbors United in Los Angeles posted signs in apartment buildings that read, "These are violence-free premises: No domestic violence."

4. **Support your local domestic violence and sexual assault centers.** Volunteer to help with hotline calls or stuffing envelopes, or become a member of a board of directors. You can also:

   - Donate clothes, household items or food for families starting lives in new violence-free homes.
   - Write a check.
   - Plan a fundraising event.
   - Lobby your local politicians to fund these essential services in your community.
   - Support rape prevention awareness campaigns in your local high school, college and community.

Resources
For names and numbers of local crisis centers, and for informational materials on community activities, call the National Victim's Center, 1-800-FYI-CALL.

41

SPEAK OUT ON VIOLENCE AGAINST WOMEN

1. **Be an impromptu educator.** Educate yourself, and then speak up. Don't sit passively when you hear victim-blaming or women-hating jokes or comments. Challenge people when you hear misinformation.

2. **Join a speaker's bureau** at your local rape crisis center, domestic violence program or other community organization that addresses these issues.

3. **Post information in likely places.** Most workplaces, apartment buildings, laundromats and other public gathering spaces have bulletin boards. Make sure information is available in all the languages spoken in your community. Post:

   ◆ Hotline numbers.
   ◆ Resource lists.
   ◆ Safe places and options for battered women.
   ◆ Places for batterers to get help.
   ◆ Information on known rapists.
   ◆ Easy-to-convey messages—for example, "no means no" or "no excuse for domestic abuse."
   ◆ Where to take self-defense classes.

4. **. . . and put information in unlikely places.** Women in one neighborhood put orange flyers into trick-or-treat bags on Halloween. The flyers told stories about battered women and teens and included an invitation to join a rape prevention group and phone numbers of local resources for help.

5. **Pressure public agencies** to promote educational information and emergency resources in creative ways. For example, domestic violence information pamphlets can be issued with marriage licenses, letting couples know that hitting a spouse is a serious crime. Police and hospitals should give out wallet-sized resource cards to the victims that they see.

> In Little Rock, Arkansas, the Women's Watchcare Network uses a group of more than 200 volunteers statewide to collect data on violence. Each year WWN tracks murders of women, especially those related to domestic violence. This information, along with information on other types of violence, is compiled annually in the Women's Watchcare Log, which is made available to the public. It lists victims' names and ages and the precise nature of the crime when available.

Resources

National Coalition Against Domestic Violence (NCADV), (303) 839-1852.

National Coalition Against Sexual Assault (NCASA), (717) 728-9781, http://www.achiever.com/freehmpg.ncas, email: ncasa@redrose.net.

42

CHALLENGE MEDIA VIOLENCE AGAINST WOMEN

Have you ever watched a movie and found yourself believing that the woman being raped was actually enjoying it? Or watched the news and wondered, what did that woman do to cause her husband to beat her? If your answer is yes, then you know how easy it is to be manipulated by media images. There are ways to challenge violent, degrading and victim-blaming images of women in the media. These images surround us and desensitize us so that sometimes we don't notice them.

1. **Heighten your awareness.** Read the newspaper. Go to a movie. Watch a TV drama. These enjoyable activities stimulate our knowledge and awareness of the world around us. While you are reading and watching, do you notice the attitudes that are reflected in the language and visual images? Pay attention. Keep yourself alert so that you don't become desensitized to real violence. Discuss this with others: your family, friends, neighbors. Challenge violence against women in your news and entertainment.

2. **Inform media people about the realities of violence against women.** For example, when news or feature articles refer to wife beating as a "domestic dispute" or "love gone awry," contact reporters, radio announcers and producers to challenge them to name the violence as it really occurred, and not to minimize its seriousness nor the effects on its victims.

3. **Don't fund violence.** Join with others to boycott films, videos and music that portray women in a sexually degrading or

violent manner. Boycott products of companies that use demeaning images of women in their advertising. Be sure to let owners and producers know about your views.

4. **Promote corporate responsibility.** Organize your friends and neighbors to pressure local companies to take responsibility for the ways they use violent or demeaning images in their billboards, newspaper and television ads and sponsorship of local events. Request meetings with company executives to discuss their commitment to using positive images of women.

> **"Hey, Bud, stop using our cans to sell yours," was the message of Dangerous Promises, a media advocacy campaign in San Francisco, San Diego and Los Angeles. The campaign used billboards and media events in an attempt to get the beer, wine and distilled spirits industries to stop using images linking women's bodies, violence and sex to sell alcohol. As a result, the wine and distilled spirits associations agreed to improve their guidelines for alcohol advertising.**

5. **Let us now praise . . . the media.** Congratulate positive characterizations, accurate information and respectful pro-gramming by sending kudos to producers and networks. Encourage the creation of heroes and heroines that use skill and brains to solve problems instead of fists and weapons. Media executives often say they give the public what they want. Let them know what you want, and that you are pleased when you get it.

Resources
Berkeley Media Studies Group offers information on media advocacy. Contact them at 2140 Shattuck Avenue, Suite 804, Berkeley, CA 94704, (510) 204-9700.

43

ORGANIZE COMMUNITY EVENTS

As 32-year-old Brad Friedman rode his bicycle into Amarillo, Texas, he was greeted by banners and news cameras. The sign on his bicycle and back said, STOP RAPE. He rode 3,000 miles coast to coast, stopping in towns and cities, raising awareness and raising money for the National Coalition Against Sexual Assault. Brad said, "I wanted to do something dramatic to stop rape." He was amazed and honored by how many people told him personal stories about themselves and their loved ones who had been raped.

Work with others in your community to organize events that bring public attention to violence against women. Invite the media and local leaders, such as politicians and business people.

1. **Organize a "town meeting,"** forum or speak-out that focuses on current concerns regarding safety for women in the community. Make sure to get media coverage.

   ♦ Invite rape survivors, formerly battered women and others affected by violence, the police chief, district attorney, advocates and others in key positions in your community.
   ♦ Facilitate a dialogue so that community members leave with a realistic view of women's safety in your community and action strategies to improve their safety.

   Several women were raped by the same rapist in Santa Monica, California, and rumors and fear spread.

Residents organized a town meeting in a neighborhood church with city officials and the police chief. As a result, self-defense classes were scheduled, and neighbors agreed to watch out for one another. Police and volunteers distributed flyers with composite drawings of the rapist. Major pressure was applied on the police department to expand their efforts to catch the rapist, and to keep the public informed about their progress.

2. **Get your marching shoes on.** Take Back the Night, Safe Homes, Safe Hoods or Stop the Violence demonstrations and marches engage community members to actively make a commitment to stand up against violence. Encourage youth, families and civic groups to attend.

3. **When silence is golden . . .** Silent witness campaigns or vigils bring to public attention the number of women who have been murdered as a result of sexual and domestic violence. Vigils are usually held at night with participants holding candles in memory of the women who have died. Silent witness campaigns visually represent the individual women who have died, with their names and stories written or sewn or otherwise documented.

The traveling "Clothesline Project" stitches women's names and their experiences with violence on T-shirts that are publicly displayed on a clothesline.

The "Silent Witness" program in Ann Arbor, Michigan, displayed life-size wood cutouts of women, with each one having a murdered woman's story on it.

44

REAL MEN DON'T HIT

To reduce violence against women, we must change the ways in which boys are raised, and often pressured, to believe that having power—and being manly—means dominating and controlling the women and girls in their lives. We must also change the ways in which girls are raised, and often pressured, to believe that a *real* woman is subordinate to her man, that she is responsible for being abused, that she "deserved it."

1. **Raise children to become nonviolent, nonvictimized adults.** Are there parenting classes at your local YMCA, YWCA or community centers? If so, check the course listings to see if classes go beyond burping and diapering. Organize or push for parenting classes and workshops that teach parents to:

   ♦ Encourage male and female children from early childhood to experience and express a full range of emotions.
   ♦ Allow their children to explore their own identities without restrictions related to gender stereotypes.
   ♦ Stimulate their children's thinking and help them develop skills for healthy relationships of all kinds, from preschool on.
   ♦ Teach problem-solving skills, conflict resolution, and other alternatives to violence.
   ♦ Teach respect.

2. **Start a Manhood Training or Rites of Passage program.** Former Harlem Globetrotter Fred McDonald's Manhood Training program grew out of lessons he learned in the streets and as an athlete and parent. He strengthens African-American and Latino young men's respect for their cultures, and teaches and supports them to develop self-respect,

mediate conflicts, manage anger, resist gangs and substance abuse and be sexually responsible and respectful of others.

3. **Bench abusive athletes.** As a community, make a statement that sexual and domestic violence are unacceptable, with clear consequences to team members who violate these rules of behavior.

Resources

There are many organizations that have developed programs designed to work with batterers on changing their abusive behavior. Four pioneers in the field are:

Abusive Men Exploring New Directions (AMEND), 777 Grant Street, Suite 600, Denver, CO 80203, (303) 832-6363.

Domestic Abuse Intervention Project (DAIP), 206 West Fourth Street, Duluth, MN 55806, (218) 722-4134.

Emerge, 2380 Massachusetts Avenue, Suite 101, Cambridge, MA 02140, (617) 422-1550.

Men Overcoming Violence (MOVE), 54 Mint Street #300, San Francisco, CA 94103, (415) 777-4496.

HATE VIOLENCE

DO YOU KNOW . . .

. . . WHAT HATE VIOLENCE IS?

◆ Hate violence is any act or attempted act to cause physical injury, property damage or emotional suffering through intimidation, harassment, bigoted slurs or epithets, vandalism, force or threat of force.

◆ Hate violence is motivated by hostility towards the victim's real or perceived ethnicity, national origin, immigrant status, gender, religious beliefs, sexual orientation, age, disability, political affiliation or any other physical or cultural characteristic.

◆ Hate violence may or may not be a crime as defined by law. When it is a criminal act motivated by hate, it is called a hate crime. Examples are: threatening phone calls, hate mail, physical assaults, cross burnings, destruction or defacing of property and firebombings.

◆ Examples of noncriminal hate violence are posting literature or posters that are demeaning, and using bigoted insults, taunts or slurs.

◆ Hate crimes based on sexual orientation continue to increase more than any other single group. In Los Angeles County, gay men are the group most often targeted by hate crimes.

◆ There has been an increase in anti-immigrant hate violence in the United States. In a significant portion of reported incidents, victims were assailed with comments such as "Go back to your country."

(Sources: Alameda County Office of Education, "Dealing with Hate-Motivated Behavior and Crime: A Call To Action," 1992; National Asian Pacific American Legal Consortium, "Audit of Hate Crimes Against Asian Pacific Americans: The Consequences of Intolerance in America," 1995; Los Angeles County Commission on Human Relations, 1994.)

45

TEACH TOLERANCE IN YOUR COMMUNITY AND SCHOOLS

A group of mothers in Chicago began talking about racial tension in their school. They decided to do some research and meet again. Within a couple of months, the parent organization (PTA) and school administrators started a tolerance education program for students and parents.

1. **Promote tolerance education.** Don't wait for an incident of racial tension to take action. Here are some ideas to get started now:

   ◆ Sensitize your school's parent organization to the multicultural interests of the students.
   ◆ Form groups to discuss racial and cultural issues in the school, such as overcoming student segregation or teaching history with cultural awareness.
   ◆ Form a committee to look at the cultural sensitivity of school books, and to raise funds to buy books on multiculturalism for the school library.
   ◆ Create opportunities in the classroom for children to learn to respect difference and appreciate diversity, and to unlearn harmful prejudices they might have already developed. Your children's schools can make use of the excellent curricula available at all grade levels, such as "Teaching Tolerance" from the Southern Poverty Law Center and "A World of Difference" from the Anti-Defamation League.

2. **Celebrate racial diversity.** Sponsor school or community events that are both educational and fun.

After an African-American home was vandalized, students, community and school leaders in Ridgewood, New Jersey, organized an annual Cultural Alladay, a special holiday for all people to honor all cultures in our society. In classes, students shared information about their cultural heritages. In assemblies, multicultural music, art and readings were featured. Daytime school forums and an evening community forum for townspeople focused on the effects of prejudice. (TEACHING TOLERANCE, Fall 1994.)

3. **If you're straight, don't assume everyone is heterosexual.** Be aware of ways gay people are discriminated against. Research has shown that people become less prejudiced when they have interactions with openly gay and lesbian people. Expand your circle of acquaintances.

In Austin, Texas, the Westlake High School newspaper ran a five-page section on gays and lesbians, and prejudice against them. The school found itself immersed in controversy. Students, parents and teachers discussed and debated ways in which gay people are demeaned. "Despite the outcry from the adults . . . in the community, the students . . . read the section with interest and little commotion. Its effect was even positive: The gay student we interviewed was elected Homecoming King," said Chip Flynn, student editor. (TEACHING TOLERANCE, Fall 1994.)

4. **Foster pride.** Share your or your family's culture and heritage and invite others to do the same. Ask teachers and community leaders to invite (to the classroom or public forums) people who may be marginalized or invisible, such as gay or lesbian parents, immigrants and disabled people. Ask them to share their histories and experiences.

5. **Can't we just get along?** Conflict resolution projects are great ways to teach ways of getting along peacefully.

Public School 321, in Brooklyn, New York, has students of diverse ethnic and class backgrounds. The school established a Peacemakers program which trains educators to teach children assertion and civility skills formally and in the daily life of the classroom. The program also trains peer mediators. Young mediators work in pairs, wearing special T-shirts and patrolling the playground and lunchroom. When they see children arguing or fighting, they approach and ask if their help is needed. The "fighters" can agree to or refuse mediation. All children in the school have a model of a successful nonviolent strategy for resolving disputes, and the mediators see themselves as peace-promoting leaders. (From Deborah Prothrow-Stith, DEADLY CONSEQUENCES, 1991.)

7. **Blow the whistle**. If you hear about a racial encounter or racial tension at your child's school or anywhere else in your community, alert school authorities or community leaders. Your involvement will make a difference. Make clear what you think the problems are and suggest ways to fix them. Form a parents' or community network to keep one another informed.

Resources

Teaching Tolerance *magazine, published by the Southern Poverty Law Center, 400 Washington Avenue, Montgomery, AL 36104.*

"A World of Difference" curriculum and materials library, Anti-Defamation League, 300 S. Dahlia Street, Suite 202, Denver, CO 80222.

"It's Elementary," a video about teaching about gays and lesbians in elementary schools, 2180 Bryant Street, Suite 203, San Francisco, CA 94110, (415) 641-4616, wemdhc@aol.com.

Diversity Tool Kit, 100 activities for diversity training by Lee Gardenschwartz and Anita Rowe, Irwin Professional Publishing,1333 Burr Ridge Parkway, Burr Ridge, IL 60521, 1-800-634-3966.

CONFLICT RESOLUTION

WHY IT WORKS:

Conflict is a normal part of human interaction.

When people take the time to explore their prejudices, they can learn how to get along with and enjoy people whose backgrounds are different.

Most disputes don't have to have a winner or loser. Win/win is the ideal way to resolve most disputes.

Children and adults who learn how to assert themselves nonviolently can avoid becoming bullies or victims.

Mediation reduces fighting and prevents violence.

HOW TO DO IT:

Discuss and define the problem from each person's point of view.

Come up with a solution together.

Choose the best idea that can work for each of you—compromise.

Implement the agreed upon solution.

46

RAISE TOLERANT KIDS

Myrlie Evers-Williams, widow of civil rights leader Medgar Evers, after enduring years of segregation, death threats and then her husband's murder by white supremacists, watched her children playing with white friends. She said, "I gradually came to the point where I did not look at another person and see their color first. And when I reached that level, it was one of the most liberating feelings I have had." Her struggle for tolerance was Mrs. Evers-Williams's greatest gift to her children (From S. Bullard, *Teaching Tolerance*, 1996).

1. **Teach tolerance by living it.** Model and discuss tolerant attitudes and beliefs about people who are different from yourself. Your children learn valuable lessons from your efforts to learn about people and to examine your own biases and prejudices.

2. **Make new acquaintances.** Your children will learn from your example. Broaden your world and cultivate new friendships. Make an effort so that you and your children get to know people of other races, sexual orientations and backgrounds.

3. **Use no discriminatory remarks or behavior.** Make sure that your children understand the power of words. By your example, and by teaching, help them understand that name-calling hurts. Set the standard for your home and your family: There's no excuse for derogatory remarks or behavior.

4. **Trace your family's history of prejudice.** Before we can serve as role models for our children, we must examine our roots

and our own experiences with prejudice. Barbara Mathias and Mary Ann French wrote in their book for parents, *Forty Ways to Raise a Nonracist Child,* "No family's history is void of prejudice or the pain of racism. If you want to understand why it is you feel the way you do about people unlike yourself, you need to [study] your family background. This [is a] very personal process." Ask yourself the following questions:

♦ When were you first aware of people unlike yourself, and what were your feelings about them?
♦ How did members of your family express their feelings about others who are different?
♦ What external factors influenced your family's opinions about others who are different?
♦ How did your family's beliefs influence your behavior?

5. **Take pride in your family's heritage, culture and background.** Give your child a sense of identity and value.

♦ Display family photos from past generations, and tell stories and memories about the people in the photos.
♦ Give your children books and videos, watch television programs and go to museums, musical events and other exhibits about your culture and cultural history (or histories if your family is multicultural). If your child's cultural background is different from your own, for example, if your child is adopted, this can be especially valuable.
♦ Make a family tree on a poster and hang it where everyone can see it.
♦ Observe family rituals, your own as well as family weddings, religious celebrations and funerals. Include principles of tolerance in your religious, cultural or other family rituals and traditions.

6. **Be aware of what your children read.** Help your children to understand that there are varied or conflicting views of history. Explain inaccurate or selective accounts of history that

reflect bias or prejudice that your children encounter in their reading or their schoolwork. Discuss the stereotypical messages they find in movies, books and computer information. Read stories, myths and fables of other cultures. Use one of these excellent multicultural bibliographies to guide you to books for your children:

♦ *Kaleidoscope: A Multicultural Booklist for Grades K–8*, National Council of Teachers of English, 1111 W. Kenyon Road, Urbana, IL 61801-1096, (217) 328-3870.
♦ *Our Family, Our Friends, Our World: An Annotated Guide to Significant Multicultural Books for Children and Teenagers*, 1991, R. R. Bowker Collection, 121 Chanlon Road, New Providence, NJ 07974, 1-800-521-8110.

Resources

Barbara Mathias and Mary Ann French, *Forty Ways to Raise a Nonracist Child, New York: HarperPerennial, 1996.*

Maureen T. Reddy, ed., *Everyday Acts Against Racism: Raising Children in a Multiracial World, Seattle: Seal Press, 1996.*

47

BE AN ALLY

Claire was at a meeting when a coworker called some-one a "fag." Claire spoke up and said, "That's a de-meaning term, plus, you're assuming he's gay because you don't think he's macho enough!" Claire is an ally.

In a management meeting, Julius said, "I don't like to hire women. The guys in Shipping have to work with two new female employees, and it's affecting morale. They can't even tell dirty jokes anymore!" Bill, manager of another division, responded by saying, "The company is changing. In my division, we came up with policies and got some training to make it an OK place to work for different kinds of people." Bill is an ally.

Cynthia was at a meeting for parents at her daughter's school. She noticed that the only two African-American mothers in a room full of white people were not joining the discussion. Based on her understanding of what it feels like to be in the minority, she asked them for their opinions. Cynthia is an ally.

An *ally* is someone who backs up others, by interrupting and intervening to stop mistreatment and correct misin-formation, lies or stereotypes they hear about them.

1. **Speak up.** Do not legitimize racial, ethnic, antigay or sexist comments, actions or jokes by your silence. Jane dreaded her family holiday gatherings because her uncle always de-meaned other racial groups in his jokes and stories, and

spoiled the gathering for her. She finally gathered the courage to ask her uncle to stop entertaining the family at the expense of others. Jane was amazed when other family members agreed with her.

2. **Don't just talk the talk—walk the walk.** Make your actions follow your beliefs. Mario refused to attend his cousin's wedding when he learned that his brother was not invited because of his interethnic marriage. He wrote a letter to his cousin, and sent copies to the entire family, explaining why he wasn't going to the wedding.

3. **Use your ASK—ability, skill, knowledge.** Use your power, knowledge and abilities as you would lend a tool, lending support. You may be privileged, for example, you don't have to worry about being oppressed because of the color of your skin, or you have an education or financial resources. Use your position to lend support, share your resources, and advocate for awareness and change. For example, Dan Li Minh, a recent immigrant, struggled to fit in at work, where he wasn't accepted by his coworkers. Bill included Dan in lunch-time socializing, and pressed his coworkers to make the adjustment easier for him.

48

MOBILIZE AGAINST HATE VIOLENCE

1. **Educate yourself.** Form a study group. Seek opportunities to talk one-on-one or in groups with others about race, class, gender and sexual orientation. Call your city's human relations commission to find out what they're doing.

   > After the Rodney King incident in Los Angeles in 1992, Thomas and Kim talked with friends about race relations in their town in Ohio. The group of friends decided they wanted to do something positive, so they invited others to join them for a barbecue and discussion. This diverse group continued to meet every Saturday for several weeks. The result was that they challenged each other by actually expressing what they really think, and formed deeper bonds that came from understanding one another's experiences.

2. Recognize and report hate crimes.

   - Research hate crime laws in your community and state. In some states, punishment is more severe when the crime has been intentionally committed against a person or group because of their race, color, religion, ancestry, national origin, disability, gender or sexual orientation.
   - Report hate crimes to police. Some criminal acts may be hate motivated. Some crimes that are more likely than others to be hate motivated are inflammatory graffiti, burning crosses, bomb threats, destruction of property, vandalism and harassment by telephone.
   - Report incidents of hate violence to community civil rights organizations that document and politically respond to trends in particular counties, states and in the country.

3. **Counteract white supremacist events.** Organize an alternate event to challenge the platform of the group or event. Use the media to project an alternative perspective to the public. Expose the hatred and racism in their message.

4. **Think before you join.** Some organizations promote positive values, but they also have intolerant or hate-filled attitudes or beliefs. Pay attention to the platforms, beliefs and values of groups that you are interested in or belong to. For example, some groups that promote pride, responsibility and self-determination also project a message of hatred towards certain others.

- Try to get the group you belong to to deal with these issues and change their attitudes and actions.
- Look critically at whether or not you want to participate in the group.

Resources

Can't We All Just Get Along? A Manual for Discussion Programs on Racism and Race Relations, *Study Circles Resource Center, P.O. Box 203, 697A Pomfret Road, Pomfret, CT 06258, (860) 928-2616, fax (860) 928-3713.*

The Los Angeles Gay and Lesbian Center Anti-Violence Project has a hotline for reporting and support for victims of antigay violence, 1-800-373-2227.

Part IV

COMMITMENT TO ACTION

49

TAKE POLITICAL ACTION

To make your world safer you may need to join others to influence policies and laws in your community. Your personal efforts count. Make sure you are well informed about the issues that concern you. Emotions are powerful motivators, but you must also have facts. Share your information and experiences with others, and together strategize the best ways to make your voices heard.

1. **Make your vote count.** Elected officials pay attention to what their constituents think. That's their job. Register to vote. Pay attention to the views and voting records of candidates and issues put forth in initiatives on the ballot. On election day, go to the polls and vote.

2. **Write a letter.** Use your telephone, fax, pen or email to communicate your message. Legislators have said that phone calls are immediate and counted, but they really pay attention to letters because of the effort that goes into them. Your letters should be brief, to the point, courteous and personal. Do not use form letters. Letters to any of the following have an impact.

   ♦ Your local politicians.
   ♦ Your state and federal legislators.
   ♦ Community relations officers of public agencies.
   ♦ The editor of your local newspaper.
   ♦ News directors of television stations.

3. **Fight city hall.** Influence elected officials, legislation and policy.

   ♦ **Show up.** You and your neighbors can attend city council meetings or public hearings to testify regarding the safety and violence prevention issues in your neighborhood.

- **Get to know your legislators and city council members.** Get to know their aides. Let them know what you think. They hold meetings and appear at public events. Make an appointment. It is mutually beneficial for them to get to know the issues in their districts.
- **Demonstrate.** Get the attention of elected officials. Organize with others to bring your concerns to the attention of people who get things done in your community. Events that dramatically demonstrate the need for violence prevention stimulate media and community members to pressure elected officials to do something about it. A peace march throughout the city or a Take Back the Park demonstration are examples of such events.

4. **Lobby for legislation.** Find out the process by which a bill becomes a law in your state. When you identify proposed legislation that helps or hurts your community, contact legislators who proposed and support it to express your support or opposition, and to find out where it is in the bill-passing process. Contact legislators and committees that are making decisions about the bill. If you would like to see new legislation introduced, contact your legislators, meet with them and talk about it. They want to hear from you.

5. **Get your story in the media.** One way to get your concerns to the attention of decision-makers is to have the media tell your story.

- **Make your message clear and concise.** Rehearse what you want to get across, and determine in advance what you want to happen.
- **Get their attention.** Contact reporters and news directors by phone and with press releases to alert them to your activities, events and ideas. If you can, develop a relationship with journalists so that they respond to you.
- **Connect reporters with authentic voices.** Reporters

respond to stories from people who actually experience violence or who have done something about it.

6. **If you can't lick 'em, join 'em.** When you encounter too little support from elected officials for your vision for your community, think about doing the job yourself. Run for office. Get appointed to a commission or committee. Sponsor a candidate you believe in.

50

MAKE A COMMITMENT TO END VIOLENCE

As you have seen, there are hundreds of actions you can take to prevent violence and promote safety. It takes the involvement of individuals, families, neighborhoods and communities. *It takes a commitment from each of us.* Violence thrives in an environment of isolation, helplessness and fear. Your commitment defeats that environment.

1. **Commitment is dedication for the long haul.** "Violence prevention is a marathon, not a sprint," said Dr. Chukwundi Saunders, Deputy Health Commissioner of Philadelphia. Preventing violence and effectively addressing all the ways in which violence affects us is a marathon effort. There are no quick fixes, but there are many contributions to be made. Don't stop after you have taken a single step, but think about what's next. Don't give up when you become discouraged, that's when commitment is tested. Think about a different approach or come up with another strategy.

2. **Commitment is personal.** Find your own ways to end and prevent violence. Your personal decisions to be aware, to refrain from using violence, to teach, speak and act reflect your willingness to participate in creating a safer world in the best way that you can. As the Vietnamese Buddhist monk Thich Nhat Hahn says, "Peace is in every step."

3. **Commitment is contagious.** Your involvement influences the people around you. As soon as you take a step to prevent violence in your environment, this affects everyone around you. When others respond to you by taking steps of their

own, independently or together, the energy to prevent violence spreads.

4. **Commitment is hopefulness.** In the face of tragedies that result from violence in our communities, our belief that violence can be prevented motivates us to take action to keep it from happening again. *Keep the faith.*

Kate Rettino

Patricia Occhiuzzo Giggans, M.A., is the Executive Director of the Los Angeles Commission on Assaults Against Women (LACAAW), a sexual assault, domestic violence and youth violence prevention center. She is the co-author, with Barrie Levy, of *What Parents Need to Know About Dating Violence*, and of the LACAAW publications *Women's Self-Defense: The Complete Guide to Assault Prevention* and *In Touch With Teens: A Relationship Violence Prevention Curriculum*. She is a Master Self-Defense trainer, has a black belt in Karate and has worked in the field of violence prevention for more than 20 years.

Rossi Studios

Barrie Levy, M.S.W., is the author of *In Love and In Danger: A Teen's Guide to Breaking Free of Abusive Relationships*, and the editor of *Dating Violence: Young Women in Danger*. Active in the movement to prevent violence against women for 25 years, she is a psychotherapist, consultant and trainer, and is on the faculty of the Departments of Social Welfare and Women's Studies at the University of California, Los Angeles.

Selected Titles from Seal Press

What Parents Need to Know About Dating Violence, by Barrie Levy and Patricia Occhiuzzo Giggans. $10.95, 1-878067-47-8. This supportive book for parents is filled with sound and comforting advice on how to recognize an abusive situation and work with their teen to end the violence.

Everyday Acts Against Racism: Raising Children in a Multiracial World, edited by Maureen T. Reddy. $15.95, 1-878067-85-0. A timely look at the impact of racism on our children and communities and what we can do about it.

In Love and In Danger: A Teen's Guide to Breaking Free of Abusive Relationships by Barrie Levy. $8.95, 1-878067-26-5. A book for teenagers about how to recognize abusive dating relationships and how to find help.

Dating Violence: Young Women in Danger, edited by Barrie Levy. $16.95, 1-878067-03-6. Includes the stories of teens and parents who've survived abusive situations, the social context of dating violence, and intervention, education and prevention strategies.

You Don't Have to Take It!: A Woman's Guide to Confronting Emotional Abuse at Work, by Ginny NiCarthy, Naomi Gottlieb and Sandra Coffman. $14.95, 1-878067-35-4. Provides practical advice and exercises to help women recognize abusive situations and respond with constructive action, including assertive confrontation and workplace organizing.

Listen Up: Voices from the Next Feminist Generation, edited by Barbara Findlen. $14.95, 1-878067-61-3. Writing with urgency and humor, these young women address racism, sexuality, identity, activism and much more.

Ordering Information

Individuals: If you are unable to obtain a Seal Press title from a bookstore, please order from us directly. Enclose payment with your order and 16.5% of the book total for shipping and handling. Washington residents should add 8.6% sales tax. Checks, MasterCard and Visa accepted. If ordering with a credit card, don't forget to include your name as it appears on the card, the expiration date and your signature.

Orders Dept., Seal Press, 3131 Western Avenue, Suite 410, Seattle, Washington 98121
1-800-754-0271 orders only
(206) 283-7844 / (206) 285-9410 fax / email: sealprss@scn.org

Visit our website at http://www.sealpress.com